W. A. (Willis Anselm) Jarrel

**The Origin, the Nature, the Kingdom, the Works, and the Destiny**

of the Devil, Together with the Devil made God's Agent

W. A. (Willis Anselm) Jarrel

**The Origin, the Nature, the Kingdom, the Works, and the Destiny**
*of the Devil, Together with the Devil made God's Agent*

ISBN/EAN: 9783337171636

Printed in Europe, USA, Canada, Australia, Japan

Cover: Foto ©Lupo / pixelio.de

More available books at **www.hansebooks.com**

THE ORIGIN, THE NATURE, THE KINGDOM,
THE WORKS, AND THE DESTINY

OF

# THE DEVIL,

TOGETHER WITH

## THE DEVIL MADE GOD'S AGENT.

Evangelist W. A. JARREL, D.D.,

Author of
"Election," "Feet Washing," "Union Meetings," "Liberty of
Conscience and the Baptists," "Old Testamen
Ethics Vindicated," "The Gospel in
Water, or Campbellism."

1892.
Published by the Author,
· Dallas, Texas.

# INTRODUCTION.

Especially for only English scholars, and more especially for the people generally, filling a place which no other book fills, this little book is published.

The importance of the subject of this book to every man and woman, the general ignorance —saying nothing of its being made a mere jest—and skepticism, in regard to it, are the reasons for its appearance.

The wide and generous reception which scholars, of Europe and America, as well as the common people, have given the author's other books, have encouraged him to write and publish this book.

The quotations, from the English Scriptures, have been made from the Revised Version, which was made by a large number of European and American scholars, and from the Common Version. Taken as a whole, in faithfulness to the originals, the Revised greatly excels the Common Version.

Praying that this humble contribution, by impressing its thousands of readers with their danger and the need of Christ to save them, may not be without a blessing to them,

Yours, in hope of a sinless life and world,

W. A. JARREL.

DALLAS, TEXAS, April, 1892.

# DEDICATION TO HIS SATANIC MAJESTY.

TO HIS SATANIC MAJESTY I ACKNOWLEDGE MY OBLIGATIONS FOR MOST OF MY EARLIEST, AND, I FEAR, SOME OF MY LATEST MORAL AND SPIRITUAL EDUCATION; TO WHOM I AM INDEBTED FOR EVERY UNLOVELY AND WICKED THING IN MY NATURE AND LIFE; FOR ALL THE PAIN, THE SORROW AND THE TROUBLE I HAVE EVER EXPERIENCED OR EVER SHALL EXPERIENCE; FROM WHOM I NEVER HAVE AND NEVER CAN RECEIVE ANY GOOD, AS HE IS HIMSELF EVIL, AND ONLY EVIL; TO WHOM I WAS ONCE ONE OF THE MOST FAITHFUL SERVANTS, BUT, WHOM, HAVING FOUND THE GOOD MASTER, WITH WHOM AND WHOSE SERVICE I AM MORE THAN DELIGHTED, I HAVE LEFT FOREVER; WHO, YET, HAS LOST NO INTEREST IN ME, AND WHOSE INTEREST IN ME LEADS HIM TO WATCH MY EVERY STEP, EVERY HOUR AND EVERY MINUTE; WHOM, CONSEQUENTLY, I HAVE TO WATCH AS I WATCH NO ONE ELSE; AND WHOM, BY THE GRACE OF JESUS CHRIST, I AM DECIDED AND DETERMINED TO CONQUER, THIS LITTLE VOLUME IS, WITHOUT ANY RESPECT OR APOLOGY, DEDICATED

BY ITS AUTHOR.

# INDEX.

## CHAPTER I.

### THE DEVIL AND DEMONS PERSONAL.

PAGE.

The Bible in plain words teaches that the devil and demons are personal ; also, in that they have minds ; moral character ; moral responsibility; in that they are punished ; and the attempt to disprove their personality implies they are personal............... 1-17

## CHAPTER II.

### ORIGIN OF THE DEVIL AND DEMONS.

God did not make them ; they had a beginning ; they made themselves ; they were once angels of heaven, and were cast into this earth for their disobedience .................................... .... 18-34

## CHAPTER III.

### THE MYSTERY OF EVIL AND OF SATAN.

The natural and the spiritual world full of mysteries. The attempt of infidelity to explain evil involves the denial and the subversion of all morality, 35-42. Science and religion essentially based on faith....... 43-46

## CHAPTER IV.
### THE NATURE AND THE NUMBER OF THE DEVIL AND DEMONS.

Meaning of the words for devil and demons in the originals, 47-51. Satan once the archangel of heaven, 53. The power and the knowledge of Satan and demons, 52-56. Their moral depravity, 56-57. Their number .................................................. 57-59

## CHAPTER V.
### SATAN'S KINGDOM.

Originated in pride; this world his kingdom; how he rules; the organization of his kingdom .......... 61-70

## CHAPTER VI.
### THE WORKS OF SATAN.

The originator of sin; puts sin into people's hearts; works miracles—the explanation of spiritism; originates false doctrines and heresies; would cause Christians to "fall from grace" if Christ did not keep them; Satan's work on bodies and minds of men producing disease, insanity and death; his reign in physical nature, affecting universal nature, producing cyclones and insect pests; treatment of disease by faith and by medicine............................ 71-96

## CHAPTER VII.
### GOD OVERRULING SATAN AND MAKING HIM HIS AGENT FOR THE GREATEST GOOD AND FOR HIS GLORY.

The Satan of the Bible independent of Persian mythology. God rules all things; Peter's fall overruled for good—not a "falling from grace"; Satan's trial of Job overruled for good; hardening Pharoah's heart—what is the meaning of that difficult Scripture —by Satan's agency and for God's glory; Satan uses the Bible as God's agent in punishing non-Bible-lovers; in producing the crucifixion Satan overruled for good; eternity will reveal God's loving and judicial designs accomplished in all Satan's works.................. 97-113

## CHAPTER VIII.
### The Final Triumph of Christ and the End of Satan and His Kingdom.

The voice of prophecy; the new earth, wherein dwelleth righteousness; the 365,000 years of the rule of Christ and His people on the earth; the Christian warfare; all evil bringing believers nearer to God; the final doom of Satan and his angels and all who do not accept Christ; eternal punishment made necessary by love, justice and righteousness; Christ the ONLY HOPE....... .. ............................ .......114-136

# CHAPTER I.

### THE DEVIL AND DEMONS PERSONAL.

Webster defines personal: "A living soul; a self-conscious being; a moral agent."

For the difference between the devil and demons, I refer the reader to Chapter IV. of this book.

1. *The Bible teaches that devil and demons are personal beings.* They are thus spoken of: "The god of this world," 2 Cor. 4:4; "Beelzebub, the chief of the devils," Luke 11:15; "the devil and his angels," Matt. 25:41; "the angel of the bottomless pit," Rev. 9:11; "the devil, and Satan the deceiver," Rev. 12:9; "the wicked one," 1 John 5:18; "a liar," John 8:44; "a murderer," John 8:44.

2. *The devil and demons having minds inevitably implies that they are personal.* Every Scripture, just quoted, to prove the devil and demons personal, clearly implies they are thinking beings; for to deceive, to lie, to murder and to all kinds of wickedness thought is necessary. Beside these statements the devil is said to have

moved David to "number" the people, 2 Chron. 21: 1; to have put it into the hearts of Ananias and Sapphira "to lie to the Holy Spirit," Acts 5: 3; to have desired to "sift" Peter, Luke 22: 31; to have "tempted" Christ, Mark 1: 13; and to deceive "the whole world," Rev. 12: 9. Satan's temptations are spoken of as "the wiles of the devil," Eph. 6: 1; his deeply laid schemes as "the depths of Satan," Rev. 2: 24. That all these expressions imply design, and that design is the act of only mind, is unquestionable. Mind means thought, moral affections and will. We, therefore, read, "that they may recover out of the snare of the devil, who are taken captive by him at his will."— 2 Tim. 2: 26. Also, that demons were among the first to recognize Christ:—"And, behold, they cried out, What have we to do with thee, thou Son of God? Art thou come to torment us before the time?"—Matt. 8: 29.

3. *The devil and demons having moral character inevitably implies they are personal.* Webster defines moral, "Relating to duty or obligation; pertaining to those intentions and actions of which right and wrong, virtue and vice, are predicated." The Scripture mentions of devil and demons, in the preceding two arguments, in-

evitably imply moral character. To illustrate that those mentions inevitably imply moral character, it is only necessary to ask the reader to turn and again read them, noticing the terms "deceiver," "liar," "murderer," "tempter," etc. All the Greek lexicons agree that the word (διάβολος—diábolos) throughout the Greek Testament rendered devil, means, "a traducer, accuser, slanderer." See Cremer's, Grimm's, Robinson's, *et om.* lexicons.

4. *The moral responsibility and the punishment of the devil and demons inevitably imply they are personal.* Besides the three preceding arguments inevitably implying the devil and demons are personal is the judgment of God on them. Of them God says, "And delivered them into chains of darkness, to be reserved unto judgment," 2 Pet. 2:4; "he hath reserved in everlasting chains under darkness unto the judgment of the great day," Jude 6; "everlasting fire, prepared for the devil and his angels," Matt. 25:41. So the demons said, "Art thou come to torment us before the time?"—Matt. 8:29.

5. *The objections to the personality of the devil and demons, and their refutation, prove Satan and his demons are personal.* In the realm of morals, from the clearest moral precept and principle

to the existence of God, there is no ground which, in the interest of some error, is not bitterly and with strong intellect and great learning contested. To find the personality or the existence of Satan and his demons not contested, would, therefore, be a great surprise. From the apostolic age to, and including the sixteenth century reformers, the personality of the devil and demons remained as the unquestionable teaching of the Bible. See Schaff-Herzog Encyc., vol. 1, p. 632. Hobbs, one of the most corrupt of the seventeenth century infidels, was the first one to push before the world the denial of the personality of the devil and demons. Followed by Lardner and Farmer, of England, and Semler, of Germany, in the eighteenth century this infidel denial was made prominent.

In the assault on the personality of Satan and his demons it is asserted, *First*, that the Scriptures mean only an evil *principle* in nature. To this assertion the reply is: (1) As principles and properties of nature are synonymous expressions, the assertion that the devil and demons are but properties of nature is anti-scientific. Of evil as a principle or property of nature, natural philosophy knows nothing. (2)

He who saves the children from Satan.—Matt. 19: 13-15

The position, that moral evil is a property of nature, is absurd to natural philosophy. Think of moral evil in stone, in metal, in a gaseous substance, in a block of wood—in any matter!! Moreover, principles or properties exert themselves blindly; but, as we have seen, the Scriptures speak of Satan and his demons acting thoughtfully and designedly. (3) The position, that moral evil is a property or principle of matter, is materialism — is infidelity. If Satan and his angels are not personal, they are not spirits. If not personal, they are properties of matter. As they think and are but properties or principles of matter, properties of matter think. That matter thinks has ever and must ever continue an essential and fundamental postulate, and one of the absurdities of the baldest infidelity. That the assumption of devil and demons being only a principle or property of matter is atheistic is clear to any right-thinking mind. For, if thought and design are principles or properties of matter, then, since God designs, God is but a principle or property of matter! Consesequently, the "orthodox" world, being the furthest extreme from infidelity, unwaveringly maintains that the devil and his demons are personal. (4) The position that moral evil is a principle or property of nature logically saps the foundation of all morality, and therefore is, in effect, the denial of the existence of sin.

If moral evil is a property of nature, since there is no moral freedom in nature, and moral freedom is necessary to moral disobedience and moral responsibility, that sin, the creature of moral evil, is the natural and necessary consequence of nature, and not of Satanic or human volition, is the inevitable conclusion. In other words, when its covering is thrown off, the position that moral evil is one of the properties of nature is but fatalism—a doctrine underlying the multifarious notions and systems noted in ethical history for their light moral tinge.

Furthermore, if moral evil is a property of nature, the converse, that moral right is a property of nature, is necessarily true. When divested of its covering, as nature has no volition and as volition is necessary to moral right, the position that moral right is a property of nature is fatalism, equivalent to the non-existence of moral right.

Making moral evil and moral right properties of nature, thus obliterating all volition, there is no possible resistance to evil or assistance to good. Hence, as the log carried by the rising current, we are to be passive to all our moral environment. As the Schaff-Herzog Encyclopedia remarks: "The denial of the personality of Satan is the first step in the denial of the sinfulness of sin. In the New Testament it is the struggle between the kingdom of Christ and the kingdom of Satan which causes apostles to glow in the description, and draws forth the vivid exhortations to fight manfully and with the armor of God, and to resist by prayer and vigilance. We may say with Dorner that the conviction of a great struggle going on between the two kingdoms of darkness and light, in which we all may take part, is adapted to produce an earnest conception of evil and develop watchfulness and tension of the moral energies."—Vol. 1, p. 632.

*Second.* While hesitating to accept the atheistic position, that moral evil and moral good are but two principles of nature, it is asserted that "Satan" and "demons" are, in the Bible, only figurative terms, indicating the evil and the good in humanity: the good as we were created; the evil as we are fallen. To this I reply: (1) Since "God hath made man upright (יָשָׁר here rendered "upright," Gesenius' Lexicon defines "upright," righteous, just; and in Deut. 32:

4; Psa. 25: 8; 92: 15, and other Scriptures, it is applied to God), Eccl. 7: 29; Gen. 1: 31, the temptation of our first parents could not have been from within themselves. As there was then no evil in nature, the inevitable conclusion is that Satan, throughout the Scriptures said to be their tempter, is not our evil nature, but the personal devil.

(2) As there was no evil within our blessed Savior ("for the prince of this world cometh, and hath nothing in me."—John 14: 30; Matt. 3: 17; Heb. 4: 15), the Satan who tempted Him could have been only the external and personal Satan.* To the position that evil is a property of matter this argument is equally applicable.

---

* Matt. 19: 17— " Why callest thou me good ? there is none good but one, that is God " – is often quoted as Christ's disclaiming immaculate character. But Adam Clarke, Geo. W. Clarke, Barnes, Matthew Henry, Stein, Roos, Nitzsch, Stier — the consensus of sound expositors is that this is not a disavowal of His holiness, but a rebuke for calling Him "good" while not accepting Him to be God, a rebuke modern infidels well deserve. For if Jesus is not what He claimed to be, He is not even "good." The new and the Bible Union versions, on the authority of the Sinaitic, the Vatican—the two most reliable MSS.—supported by the consensus of textual critics, read this: "Why askest thou me concerning good? One there is who is good."

(3) As there is no sinful nature in hogs, and as they can not take sin or insanity from human beings, the demons which entered into the swine, from the demoniac who lived in the tombs, could have been only personal beings. Matt. 8: 32.

*Third.* The attempt to explain away the personalities of Satan and his demons is only the pettifogger in the Scriptural court. Satan and his demons being, in the Bible, spoken of in terms and phrases which as clearly denote personality as the Bible terms and phrases which speak of God and His angels denote personality, as well assume that God and His angels are only "properties of matter," or the "good in our natures," as to assume that Satan and his angels are the moral properties of matter, or the evil within us. Such perversions of the Scriptures are a great sin, a mockery of God, and violate the rules of interpretation governing the interpretation of both uninspired and inspired writings. Says Blackstone: "Words are generally to be understood in their usual and most known signification; not so much regarding the propriety of grammar as their general and popular use."—Blackstone's Com., vol. 1, pp. 59-61.

Says Moses Stuart: "All men, in their daily conversation and writings, attach but one sense to a word, at the same time and in the same passage, unless they design to speak in enigmas."

Horne says: "The meaning of a word used by a writer is the meaning affixed to it by those for whom he immediately wrote. The received (or most obvious) signification of a word is to be in all cases retained unless weighty and necessary reasons require that it should be abandoned. In no case may we select a meaning repugnant to natural reason."

Morus, approvingly quoted by Ernesti: "There can be no certainty at all in respect to the interpretation of any passage unless a kind of necessity compels us to affix a particular sense to a word; which sense, as I have before said, must be one; and unless there are special reasons for a tropical (or secondary) meaning, it must be the literal sense."

Ernesti: "The primary or literal meaning is the true one."

(1) With the Lexicons agreed that the terms for devil and demons denote personal beings; (2) the people among whom the Bible was written, to whom it was spoken and by whom it was

The whisky traffic makes this little child sleep on the bare and cold floor.

accepted, believing there were a personal devil and demons; (3) the personality of Satan and his demons the belief of the Christian world until and including the sixteenth century Reformation; (4) the orthodox world to and including the present believing Satan and his demons personal; (5) the absurdity and the mockery of the resorts to explain away the plain Scripture statements, that Satan and his demons are personal — all these, in the light of the above rules of interpretation, make the personalities of the devil and his angels as certainly the teachings of the Scriptures as the personalities of God and His angels are their teachings.

*Fourth.* But here we are met with the answer: "We admit that the Bible terms and phrases, concerning devil and demons, mean that they are personal beings, but Jesus only accommodated Himself to the weakness and the ignorance of the people of His age."

To this I reply: (1) Jesus was tempted by the devil or He was not; the demons went out of the man into the swine or they did not. If the devil tempted Jesus and demons entered the swine, the Bible is historically true; if not, historically false. As the account of the temptation of Jesus and the swine, clearly, is not a reference or an allusion to the views of the people, but is a statement of a real occurrence, that account most unequivocally reports the doings of the personal devil and his personal demons.

(2) If the belief that Satan and his demons are personal is "superstitious," by accommodating Himself to that view Jesus indirectly indorsed a "superstition"; and, as He knew the result of that indorsement, He stamped his indorsement upon a "superstition" for all future ages—for the time will never come when Jesus will not be understood as teaching the personality of the devil and his angels. In other words, if the devil and demons are not personal, Jesus, by example and teaching—by pretending to "cast out devils," by addressing them as personal, and by commissioning his disciples to "cast out devils"—intentionally deceived the people for all time. See Matt. 4: 24; 8: 16, 31; Mark 1: 32; 5:12; 9:38; Luke 9: 1; 10: 17; 13: 32. In the language of Smith's Bible Dictionary, vol. 4, p. 2848: "The New Testament brings it (the personality) plainly forward. From the beginning of the Gospel, when he appears as the personal tempter of our Lord, through all the Gospels, Epistles and Apocalypse, it is asserted or implied, again and again, as a famil-

iar and important truth. To refer this to mere 'accommodation' of the language of our Lord and his apostles to the ordinary Jewish belief is to contradict facts and evade the meaning of words. The subject is not one on which error could be tolerated as unimportant; but one important, practical and awful. The language used respecting it is either truth or falsehood; and unless we impute error or deceit to the writers of the New Testament we must receive the doctrine of the existence of Satan as the doctrine of Revelation."

To conclude this argument without calling attention to how this "accommodation" wickedness seeks to make havoc with Christianity would be wrong. In getting rid of eternal punishment, of demoniacal possession, of Jona being swallowed by the whale, of the ark and the flood, of Moses and the brazen serpent, of the incarnation, of the angelic ministry to the saints and other great Scripture truths, the "accommodation" subterfuge figures as extensively as in getting rid of the personal existence of the devil and his angels. In truth, to conceive of any doctrine of revelation which can not be eliminated by the "accommodation" wickedness would be very difficult, if not impossible. In defending the so-called "higher criticism," as represented by Kuenen, Wellhausen, Steck, Pfleiderer and company, the accommodation theory is the main refuge. The advocates of this so-called "higher criticism," like these infidel deniers of the personality of Satan and his angels, when pressed with the truth, that Jesus indorsed the Old Testament books as the books of Moses, etc., say He only "accommodated" Himself to the prevalent belief among the Jews.

Better take the out-and-out infidel resort of Paulus and company, that Jesus and his apostles while teaching the personality of Satan and his demons did so from partaking of the ignorance and the superstition of their age. For, while the "accommodation" subterfuge, the moral evil as a property of matter subterfuge, and the subterfuge that the devil and demons are our fallen nature, reflect on the moral nature of Christ and sap the basis of all morality, the Paulus subterfuge, while historically and philosophically baseless, does not impeach the moral character of Christ, but only his knowledge. Thus here, as everywhere else, open infidelity is not so dangerous as that which seeks to hide itself under the garb of Christianity—as that which "steals the livery of heaven in which to serve the devil."

With no doubt that every candid and reasonable man, willing to yield to the plain teachings of the Holy Scriptures, after studying prayerfully this chapter, will believe that the Holy Scriptures teach there are a devil and demons, I ask the reader to prayerfully follow me through the succeeding chapters of this book.

# CHAPTER II.

### ORIGIN OF THE DEVIL AND DEMONS.

The questions are asked: "Did God make the devil and demons?" "Did they make themselves?" "Or, are they eternal?"

1. *God did not make the devil and demons.* Only in the sense that God providentially permits evil, and so governs the world as to send it on men, does He create evil. See and compare Isa. 45: 1–7, especially verses 1 and 7; also, compare 2 Sam. 24: 1 with 1 Chron. 21: 1.* Not only is this the certain teaching of the Holy Scriptures, but, since making God the

---

* In verse 10 of 1 Sam. 24, it is recorded that, for numbering the people, "David's heart smote him," and that he confessed to the Lord, "I have sinned greatly in what I have done." His numbering them was confiding in flesh instead of in the Spirit. For David's pride, through Satan's agency, as God overturns Satan's devices to his own glory, He moved David to number the people. So, 2 Sam. 24: 1, says God moved Satan to do so, while 1 Chron. 21: 1, speaking of Satan as God's agent, says Satan led David to number the people. Booth, Boyd, Davidson and Hervey render 2 Sam. 24: "An adversary stood up against Israel." And Hervey thinks some unnamed person so moved David.

originator of sin would impeach His holiness, it is equally the plain teaching of reason.

2. *Satan and his demons had a beginning.* In the sense of having no beginning only God is eternal. The following Scriptures admit of no interpretation excluding the truth that only God has no beginning: "The high and lofty one that inhabiteth eternity."—Isa. 57: 15. "The eternal God is thy dwelling place."—Deut. 33: 27. "His everlasting power and divinity."—Rom. 1: 20. "The King eternal, incorruptible, invisible, the only God."—1 Tim. 1: 17. "Blessed be the Lord, the God of Israel, from everlasting to everlasting."—Psa. 41: 13. "Before the mountains were brought forth, or ever thou hadst formed the earth and the world, even from everlasting to everlasting, thou art God."—Psa. 90: 2. "Thou art from everlasting."—Psa. 93: 2. "Our Redeemer, from everlasting is thy name."—Isa. 63: 17. "Whose goings forth are from old, from everlasting."—Micah 5:2. "The everlasting God."—Gen. 21: 33. "The everlasting God, the Lord, the Creator of the ends of the earth."—Isa. 48: 28. "The commandment of the eternal God."—Rom 16: 26 The Hebrew (עוֹלָם) word for ev-

erlasting and eternal, in all these Scriptures, says Gesenius' Lexicon, expresses "the true and full idea of eternity." The phrase in Isa. 57: 15 (שֹׁכֵן עַד) Gesenius' Lexicon thus defines, "inhabiting eternity, sitting enthroned forever." The New Testament words, in the foregoing quotations, are the (ἀίδιος, αἰών, αἰώνιος) only Greek words for endlessness. Thus Cremer's Biblico-Theological Lexicon of the Greek New Testament defines "constant, abiding, eternal." Grimm's New Testament Greek Lexicon: "Without beginning or end, that which always was and always will be, Θεός, (God)."—Rom. 16: 26.†

Again, God says: "I am Alpha and Omega, the first and the last, the beginning and the end."—Rev. 21: 13. (Alpha and Omega are the first and the last letters of the Greek alphabet)

Concluding this argument:—The Scriptures clearly teaching that only God has no beginning settle that Satan did not always exist.

---

† In view of these being the only Greek words for endless time, and their being used for the endless felicity of the righteous, as well as for God's endlessness, how unscriptural and wicked for any one to attempt to prove the punishment of the lost will ever end! See Matt. 18: 8; 25: 46.

This will further appear, under the next argument.

3. *Satan and his angels made themselves Satan and demons.* In the Holy Scriptures we read: "For if God spared not the angels when they sinned, but cast them down to hell, and committed them to pits of darkness, to be reserved unto judgment."—2 Pet. 2: 4. "And angels which kept not their own principality, but left their proper habitation, he hath kept in everlasting bonds under darkness unto the judgment of the great day."—Jude 6.

From these fallen angels being cast into the place where the devil and his demons are and from the devil and demons, in other Scriptures, being mentioned as fallen creatures, that the fallen angels are the devil and demons is certain.

(1) *Tartaroō* (ταρταρώσας) in Pet. 2: 4, rendered "cast them down to hell," occurs nowhere else in the New Testament, nor in the Septuagint. Says Adam Clarke: "It appears from a passage in Lucian that by *tartaros* (ταρταρος) was meant, in a physical sense, the bounds or verge of the material system." Supporting this, Clarke translates and quotes from Lucian: "Thou formedst the *universe;* . . . . thou drovest it to the confines or recesses of our outer *Tartarus.*"

Commenting on an expression from Hesiod, a Greek poet, Clarke says: "So it must not be dissembled that the Greeks speak of *Tartarus* as a vast pit or gulf in the bowels" of the earth. Then, from Hesiod, Clarke quotes, translating:

"Black Tartarus within earth's spacious womb."

From Homer Clarke quotes:

"O far, O far, from steep Olympus thrown,
 Low in the deep *Tartarean* gulf shall groan,
 That gulf which iron gates and frozen ground
 *Within the earth* inexorably bound."

Clarke concludes: "On the whole, then, *tartaroun* (ταρταρουν) in St. Peter, is the same as *riptein es Tartaroun* ('ριπτειν ες ταρταρουν), to throw into Tartartus, in Homer, only rectifying the poet's mistake of *Tartarus* being in the bowels of the earth, and recurring to the original sense of that word above explained, which, when applied to spirits, must be interpreted *spiritually;* and thus *tartarosas* (ταρταροσας) will import that God cast the apostate angels out of his presence into that *zophos tou skotous* (ζοφος του σκοτους)—blackness of darkness (2 Pet. 2: 17; Jude, 5, 15), banished *from the light of his countenance,* and from the *beautifying influence of the ever blessed Three,* as truly as a person

plunged into the *torpid* **boundary of this created system** would be from the *light of the sun* and the benign operations of the material heavens."
—Adam Clarke *in loco*.

In the classics *Tartarus* is also sometimes used differently from the above. But Adam Clarke is so correct as to *Tartarus* meaning this earth, in contrast with "the light of his countenance" and the "beautifying influence of the ever-blessed Three," that, after otherwise defining it, Liddell and Scott's Lexicon closes its explanation of the word by saying, " probably to express *something terrible.*" In the same line Scott's Commentary says: "The meaning of it must not be sought from the fables of the Greek poets, but from the general tenor of the Sacred Scriptures"—*in loco*. After wandering around in the tombs of the Greek poets for the meaning of *Tartarus,* Bengel concedes and concludes: "But it is possible for slaves of *Tartarus* to dwell also on the earth (Luke 8: 31; Eph. 2: 2; Apoc. 9: 11, 14; 12: 9, etc.), just as it is possible for one taken captive in war to walk even beyond the place of captivity"—*in loco*.

Dr. Wm. Ramsey, a learned writer, says: "The word *Tartarus* means, according to Greek writers, in a *physical sense*, the bounds or verge of this material system. . . . ‹ That place is probably, at present, within the atmosphere of our earth."

Suidas, an ancient writer, says *Tartarus* signifies "the place in the clouds," or, "in the air."

Grotius, a very learned writer: "That is called *Tartarus* which is lowest in anything; whether in the earth, or in the water, or, as here, in the air."

Bishop Whately, a most learned classical, metaphysical and Episcopal scholar: "The word used by Peter, which our translators render 'cast down into hell,' or *Tartarus*, is to be understood of our dark, gloomy earth, with its dull clouds, foul vapors, and misty atmosphere. . . . . Socrates called the abyss, or sea, *Tartarus*, as does also Plato, who elsewhere calls our dim, lack-luster earth itself, also, *Tartarus*. Plutarch says our air . . . . is called *Tartarus*, from being cold. Herein he is followed and supported by Lucian. And both Hesiod and Homer call it the 'aerial *Tartarus*.' In no other sense or way can St. Peter be understood or explained. Lucian says: 'The great depth of the air is called *Tartarus*.'"

Training young lips to sing for Jesus instead of for Satan.

Ralph Cudworth, of whose writing and of whom the Schaff-Herzog Encyclopedia says: "The enormous learning of the book has hindered its usefulness;" "Cudworth is a storehouse whence most precious material has been taken by many a lesser writer. . . . . He was the leader of the Cambridge Platonists "—Cudworth says, of 2 Pet. 2: 4: "And by *Tartarus* here, in all probability, is meant this lower caliginous (*i. e.*, dark) air, or atmosphere of the earth, according to that of St. Austin, concerning these angels, ' That after their sin, they were thrust down into the misty darkness of this lower air.' "—Cudworth's Intellectual System, vol. 3, p. 363.

These authorities, to which others can be added, sufficiently prove that *Tartarus*, into which the fallen angels were cast, is not hell, but the earth; and they also prove that lexicons and others, giving the word the meaning of only "hell," have too closely followed only *some* of the Greek writings, and, especially, where they use the word in the spiritual sense, while Peter uses it in the material. In this is seen, probably, the significancy of the Septuagint not using *Tartarus* for hell.

(2) These fallen angels being "reserved" "unto the judgment of the great day" (2 Pet. 2: 4 ; Jude 6), also proves that *Tartarus* does not mean hell. That they are "reserved" unto that awful judgment, from which the lost are sent into hell, is too Scripturally evident for argument to be here necessary.

(3) Says Jesus: "I beheld Satan fallen as lightning from heaven."—Luke 10: 18. (Most quotations in this book are from the Revised Version.)

Says Stier: "But, inasmuch as it is immediately connected by ὡς with σατανᾶν (the first Greek word here means "as," or like, the second is Satan), it contains, at the same time, hidden reference to the bright character of an angel of light, possessed by the fallen spirit, when he was yet in heaven. And herein we find also the first answer to the question : *When was it that the Lord saw Satan fall from heaven?*" —Words of Jesus, vol. 3, p. 491.

Hoffman: Yes, the Lord here speaks as a "Witness of what happened to Satan in the primal beginning," Erasmus: "*Insignis erat illius dignitas in coeliis*"—in other words, Erasmus says the passage alludes to Satan's former greatness in heaven. So D. S. Schaff, *et al.*

(4) *Of the devil's origin Jesus says: "He was a murderer from the beginning, and stood not in the truth, because there is no truth in him."—John 8: 44.

As Stier comments (Words of Jesus, vol. 5, p. 385), Jesus here speaks of "the beginning of human history, from the time when men were for him to murder, since he first—who already before existed ($\mathring{\eta}\nu$), appeared and attacked the

---

*Excepting when misled by mistranslations, to any one who has thoroughly investigated the Scriptures on the subject, it is very clear that neither human souls nor souls of the fallen angels are now in hell. From the New Testament Greek, besides ταρταρόω (*tartaroō*) there are two words in our version rendered "hell," *gehenna* and *hadees* (γεέννα, ᾅδης). While, as in the case of the rich man, *hadees*, designating the intermediate world, in which the righteous and the wicked remain until their resurrection (which is divided into a place of felicity and a place of misery), designates a place of punishment. That place is not *gehenna* or hell.

Into the happy department of *hadees* Jesus went with the thief on the cross; from it He arose and went to heaven. From that happy part of *hadees* Lazarus looked across into the part of *hadees* where lost souls are. It is *hadees* instead of *gehenna*, the word for hell, which "delivered up the dead," and which "were cast into the lake of fire," instead of hell cast into hell, as the Revised Version absurdly reads.—Rev. 20: 13-15. No devils in *hadees* or in *gehenna*—only in *Tartarus*, but, finally, lost souls now in *hadees* and fallen angels in *Tartarus* together go into *gehenna*.—Matt. 25: 41.

human race." So Tholuck, Harless, Bengel, Adam Clarke, Matthew Henry, Luther, Lyser, Krabbe, Tittman, Gerhard, Julius Muller, Olshausen, Paulus, Kuinoel, Meyer, Fromman, Calvin, Origen, Augustine, Crysostom, Theophylact, *et mul. al.*

*See, also, John 1: 1, 2; 1 John 3: 8. The phrase, "from the beginning," is, therefore, to be dismissed, as not stating that Satan, from his beginning as a creature, was a murderer.

The words which state that Satan is a fallen being are "*stood* not in the truth " (ἐν τῇ ἀληθείᾳ οὐχ ἕστηκεν). Says Tholuck: "*"Ἕστηκεν* (*hesteeken* is the Greek, rendered "stood"), by the Vulgate, Luther and all the expositors down to Bengel (by v. Cöln, also Bibl. Theolog. ii. 71), is taken as the preterit, and the passage has consequently been taken as a dictum probans (proof-text) for the fall of the devil, 2 Pet. 2: 4."—*in loco*.

Bengel: " Οὐχ ἕστηκεν, he abode not (did not stand fast). . . . He did not attain a fixed

---

*In allowing the passage this meaning, but attempting to so explain it so as to make Satan the instigator of Cain's murder, Doederlein, Nitzsch, Lucke, Schulthess, De Wette, Koostlin, Reuss, Cyrill, Kling are, perhaps, going too far. Of course, Satan instigated that murder, but Jesus hardly mentions that.

standing in the truth. (A similar expression occurs in Rom. 5: 2, "We have access by faith into the grace wherein we have obtained an established standing.") . . . . *There was* truth in him; but *there is not now.* Moreover, when the first truth ceased to exist in him, it was by his own fault."—*in loco.*

Regarding Christ as here revealing the fall of Satan, Neander says: "Lie and sin having become his *second* nature, he *stands* not in the truth, and can find no resting-place there."

V. Gerlach: "He finds no footing, no resting-place in the truth, because his inmost being is *alienated* from it."

Lange: "He did not stand in the truth."

Beck: "One who did not establish himself and take his position in the truth of life."

Olshausen: "We must be driven to a view of the very words very similar to the ancient interpretation of Satan's apostasy; and this admits of a grammatical vindication. $Ἔστηκε$ (rendered stood) has the signification of *enduring*, as Lücke and Tholuck acknowledge. The declaration . . . does not, indeed, expressly assert his fall, but contains it implicitly. Only that the fall is not so much an isolated fact, but as a continuous conduct and state."

Nitzsch concedes that οὐχ ἔστηκεν (rendered stood not) points to a fact apart from the history of the fall (fall of man), and of the domain of history generally."

Martensen: "This beginning of his fall it is which the Lord here hints at when he says that the devil did not abide in the truth."

Stier: "We can not but trace in the origination of that use of the word . . . the notion of an *abiding* in a former fixed place . . . . He is *in fact*, as all his deeds and words from the beginning show, bare of all truth; this is the evidence of an οὐχ ἔστεχεν (abode not), of a falling at his beginning into that condition from another; and so 'not' is almost an equivalent to 'no longer.'" So Augustine, Lampe, Harless, Lyser, Piscator, Matthew Henry, Adam Clarke, D. S. Schaff, *et mul. al.*

In view of the language of John 8: 44 and the way this mass of interpreters understand it, in using it, to prove the fall of Satan, I feel that I stand on solid rock.

(5) The fallen angels having been assigned to and cast into the earth, until sent to hell, and the devil and his demons, also, dwelling here, in view of the truth that there are no other

Satan makes unhappy children.

evil spirits, not human, on earth, we necessarily conclude that the devil and demons are the angels which "kept not their first estate."

That the devil and demons are fallen angels is the plain Bible teaching, I feel certain every reader, who has prayerfully and carefully followed me through this chapter will conclude.

I will close this chapter by noticing the question: "How did the devil and demons make themselves?"

In answer (1), not in the sense of creation. God created them angels. (2) They made themselves devil and demons by sinning. Just as God never made the sinner, but made man righteous, and by sinning he made himself a sinner; just as God never made a thief, a robber, a murderer, but made them men, and, by crime, they made themselves liars, thieves and murderers. "Sin is the transgression of the law."—1 John 3: 4. To say, therefore, that God made the sinner is to absurdly say that He made man transgress the law. As the devil, by transgression, became the sinner, and as the only difference between fallen and unfallen angels is, the former are sinners while the latter are obedient, it is evident that by sin Satan and his demons became "devils." To further illustrate: God made Adam and Eve righteous, but, by disobedience, they made themselves sinners. Again, of the heathen it is said: "And changed the glory of the uncorruptible God into an image made like to corruptible man."—Rom. 1: 23. Just as God did not make these idolaters, but made them men and women, and as they, by changing "the glory of the uncorruptible God into an image made like to corruptible man," made themselves idolaters, so God made angels, and, by sinning, they made themselves "devils" and "demons."

That the devil and demons have not always existed, that God did not make them but that they made themselves, is scripturally certain and reasonable.

## CHAPTER III.

THE MYSTERY OF EVIL AND OF SATAN.

To enter into an extended discussion of how a pure being, with no sin in existence to tempt him, could sin, a matter on which the Holy Scriptures are silent, and which discussion would make a large book, is not my purpose. But there is a shallow, infidel, so-called, "attempted" explanation of the origin of sin, which, while professing great profundity, is profound only as to its wickedness and absurdity, which must not here pass unexposed. That attempted explanation is: "Everything must have its counterpart." This proposition is attempted to be sustained by such arguments as, "day implies night; large implies small; white implies black; ease implies pain, etc. In reply (1), that there can be day without night; large without small; white without black; and ease without pain, are too self-evident to require proof. While relatively necessary, darkness, smallness, blackness and pain are, therefore, not absolutely necessary. (2) Inasmuch as only pain, among these things, is an evil, the introducing "black," "small" and "night" into the argument is misleading. (3) The argument is based on analogy, and, as all logicians agree that arguments from analogy are unreliable, the argument is, therefore, unsatisfactory. (4) The argument is contradictory to reason. As well say, oppression is necessary to freedom; foolishness to wisdom; hunger to satiety; weakness to strength; hate to love; drunkenness to soberness; blindness to sight; licentiousness to virtue; lying to truthfulness; murder to love; covetousness to liberality; dishonesty to honesty; idolatry to worship of God; as to say sin is necessary to righteousness and Satan to God. (5) This explanation of the origin of sin and Satan obliterates all moral distinction and "turns hell loose on the earth." As night is as legitimate as day; small as large; black as white, so, on this infidel attempted explanation of the origin of evil, all wickedness would be as legitimate as righteousness. In a debate, in 1872, with an infidel, I had to meet his attempted justification of all sin and crime, on the counterpart theory. So, in the "Banner of Light," of December 3, 1862, a Boston infidel paper, we read a report of an infidel prayer:

Unless it early gives its heart to Jesus, who knows what Satan will make of this little child?—Eccl. 12: 1.

"We thank thee for all conditions of men, for the drunkard, for the prostitute, for the dissolute of every description."

In the same paper, of January 18, 1862, we read: "I have no reply for those who tell me such a one does wickedly, or such a one holds erroneous sentiments; that one is in free love and another in atheism; for there is not an act done, not a sentiment entertained, not a freak of free love, nor a frozen blast of atheism, . . . . that does not help on the grand and glorious superstructure." In the same paper, of March 8, 1862, we read: "There never was a spirit that trespassed upon the smallest portion of God's law." In the same paper, of October 29, 1859, we read from a report of an infidel speech, in an infidel convention: "That which we call sin and evil in human actions is a necessity, and being a necessity is lawful and right."

Haeckel, the ablest German infidel scientist: "Between the most highly developed animal souls and the lowest human souls, there exists only small quantitative, but no qualitative, difference."—Haeckel's Hist. Creation, vol. 2, p. 362.

Carl Vogt, another representative infidel German scientist: "The distinguishing between morally good and evil action is merely self-deception."—Wuttke's Ethics, vol. I, p. 355.

Moleschott, another German infidel: "To comprehend everything involves also the justifying of everything."—*Idem et ibid.*

B. F. Underwood, one of the ablest living American infidels: "The materialist (the infidel) maintains that good and evil are only relative terms. . . . Man has learned in the school of experience what promotes his happiness and what diminishes his enjoyments. The one he calls good, the other evil."—Materialism, by Underwood, pp. 14, 15.

Hume, in whom English Deism reached its climax: "General and necessary moral ideas there are none; hence, moral conceptions have always a varying worth and rest essentially on custom."—Wuttke's Ethics, vol. I, p. 212.

Hobbes, one of the most eminently representative infidel writers, thought that whatever was not "prescribed by the king is morally indifferent."—Macaulay's History of England, vol. I, p. 53; Leckys' History of European Morals, vol. I, pp. 11, 122.

Dryden, an infidel poet, wrote:

"Why should a foolish marriage vow,
  Which long ago was made,
Oblige us to each other now,
  When passion has decayed?
We loved, and we loved as long as we could,
  Till our love was loved out of us both;
But our marriage is dead
When the pleasure is fled;
  'Twas pleasure first made it an oath."

Writing to a female friend, Pope, another infidel poet, exhorts her—

"Not to quit the free innocence of life
For the dull glory of a virtuous life."

—Reed's History of English Literature, pp. 227-237.

From the New York "Ledger," of May 1. 1880, I clipped the following, from its question column: "I am an infidel, and glory in my mental freedom. I pity all who are bound with the galling yoke—religious superstition. I have a wife whom I once loved, but long ago that feeling left me. She is an invalid, and the doctor says she can not live more than a year. Now, there is a lady in this neighborhood whom I do love, but she is sought after by other suitors; and I am afraid if I do not manage in some way to free myself pretty soon, she will be lost to me forever, and I will be rendered most miserable. As things are, two lives are made unhappy; she would be free from her intense pain, and I made free. Why could I not administer to her some poison that would send her quietly off? Would I not be justified in so doing?"

Of infidelity—the doctrine which holds evil essential to good—Bancroft, the great American historian, wrote: "Good government is not the creation of skepticism. Her garments are red with blood, and ruin is her delight; her despair may stimulate to voluptuousness and revenge, she never kindled with the disinterested love of men."—Bancroft's History of the United States, vol. 5, pp. 22, 24—old edition.*

---

*For a thorough *expose* of infidel immorality, the reader is referred to "Old Testament Ethics Vindicated," by the author of this little work. It has near 300 pages, well printed and bound in cloth, and sent to any address by the author on receipt of $1.50, at his address, Dallas, Tex. It is highly recommended by more than a hundred of the most eminent European and American scholars. Of the work, the Cincinnati "Gazette" says: "The author is well up in the literature of the subject, and cites freely from writers of every variety of opinion, and battles valiantly for the Old Testament as in every way superior to the sacred books of

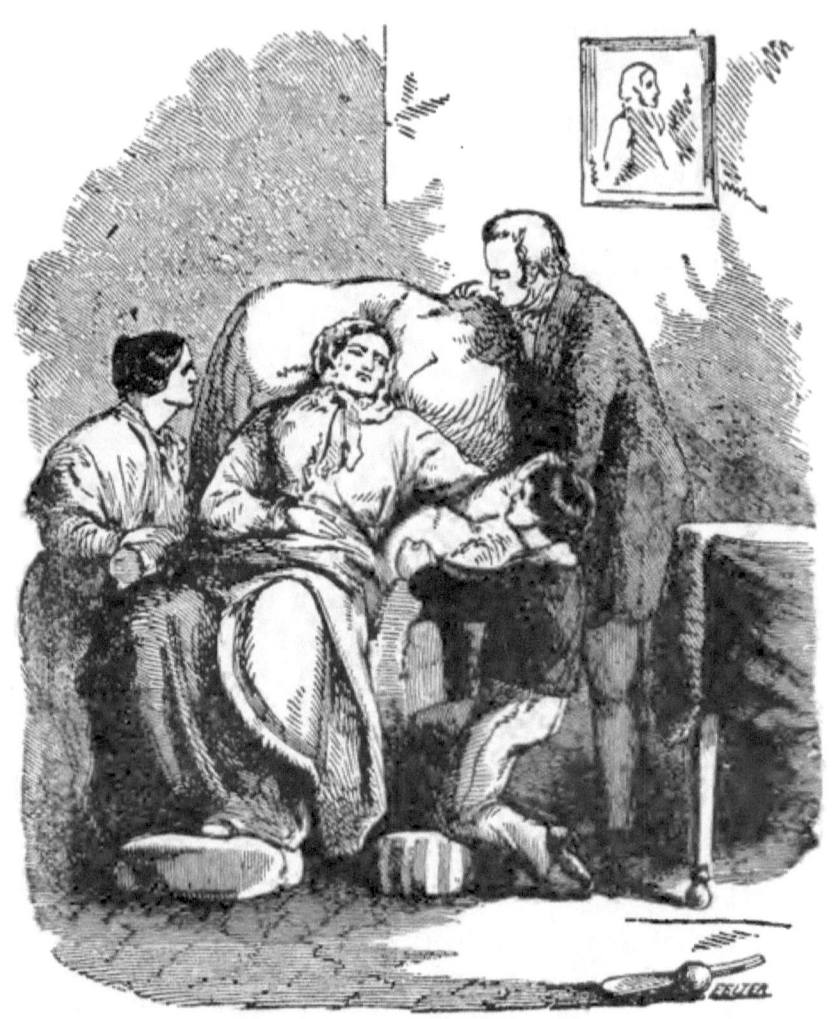

The little boy promising his dying mother to meet her where the devil never can enter—in heaven.

Having annihilated the counterpart or correspondence theory of the origin of sin, because of its havoc on morality, we must be content to go no further into its origin than we did in the last of Chapter II. of this book. Any one who desires an extended discussion of the origin of sin will find no work so reliable and thorough as the "Christian Doctrine of Sin," by Julius Müller, in two large volumes.

Greg, one of the most thoughtful of English infidel essayists, well says of the mystery of evil: "It has scattered those who have tried to master it as widely as the . . . tower of Babel. Some it has driven into atheism, some into Manichæism, some into the denial of the most obvious facts of life and nature, some into the betrayals of the most fundamental principles of morality."—Enigmas of Life, p. 17.

Müller says: "Weisse rightly regards the conflict between freedom and necessity to be the main problem of philosophy in its imme-

---

the heathen and to the theories of modern unbelievers. It is decidedly refreshing in these days of timid compromise to find one so firm in his opinion and who gives so much good reason for the facts. . . . No one can object when Ingersoll and his imitators are flayed alive with their own weapons."

diate future."—Christian Doctrine of Sin, vol. 2, p. 131.

God has two great books—the one the Book of Nature, the other the Bible. On every page of the Book of Nature, as in the Bible, man runs into the fathomless mystery. In each he finds sufficient light for life.

As to the Book of Nature: Why make disease and remedy for disease? Why poisons and their antidotes? Why the rats and the mice, and the cats to catch them? Why not leave unmade the evils, and then no necessity for the instruments to remove them? Thus, scarcely have we glanced into the Book of Nature than we find the same mysterious handwriting which so puzzles us in the Book of Revelation.

Says Milner: "The scrutinizing eye of science penetrates with far-reaching sight the system of things about us, and in the dim limits of its vision reads the word 'mystery.'"

Herbert Spencer, an infidel: "The man of science, more than any other, knows that in its ultimate essence nothing can be known."

Faraday, the father of the science of electricity: "I once thought I knew something about electricity, but the more I investigated it the less I found I understood it."

Prof. Tyndall, an infidel: "Between molecular mechanics and consciousness is interposed a fissure, over which the ladder of physical reason is incompetent to carry us."

Prof. Haeckel, an infidel: "What do we know certainly of the essential nature of matter and force? What of gravitation? What of the essential nature of electricity, or the imponderables generally, whose very existence is not proved? What of ether, upon which our formal science of light and optics is founded; and what of the atomic theory on which our chemistry is built? We do not certainly know these things."

Wisely did Simonides answer the King of Syracuse for a definition of God, so impliedly related to the origin of evil: "The more I think of Him, the more He is unknown to me."

As the sweetest of American poets, Whittier. sings:

> " Who fathoms the eternal thought?
> Who talks of scheme and plan?
> The Lord is God! He needeth not
> The poor device of man.
>
> " I dimly guess from blessings known
> Of greater out of sight;
> And with the chastened Psalmist own
> His judgments, too, are right."

As we have seen, God has told us there are devil and demons, their origin—and as we shall see—their nature, where they are, work, and their destiny. But more than that He has left concealed.

As the man of science, as we have just seen, bases his science essentially upon FAITH and receives mysteries because they ARE, and not because he *understands* them, so does the Christian, in the realm of spiritual things. As it is the triumph of reason for the man of science to walk by *faith*, so the Christian's walk by faith is the highest triumph of reason. In either case only foolishness tremblingly or scoffingly refuses to walk.

To the novice who refuses to believe the Bible because, like nature, mystery is its every page, and who, from a *little* reading and thought, imagines himself wonderfully wise, is commended:

> "Little learning is a dangerous thing;
> Drink deep or taste not the Pierian spring.
> Light draughts intoxicate the brain;
> Drink deep and you are made sober again."

# CHAPTER IV.

## THE NATURE AND THE NUMBER OF THE DEVIL AND DEMONS.

While the personality of Satan is taught in the Old Testament, as it is but the New Testament in germ, and also, as Trench says, "till the mightier power of good was revealed, were we in mercy not suffered to know how mighty the power of evil: and even here it is in each case only to the innermost circle of the disciples that the explanation concerning Satan is given. . . . . And instead of hearing less of Satan, as the mystery of the kingdom of God proceeds to unfold itself, in the last book of Scripture, that which details the fortunes of the Church till the end of time, we hear more and more of him."—Trench on the Parables, p. 79.

1. *Satan and his demons.* (1) The Old Testament word for the arch-fiend is שָׂטָן, English, Satan. The word Satan, in Hebrew, means adversary and is applied to any one whom the writer or speaker was pleased to denominate an

adversary. But "with the article הַשָּׂטָן the adversary χατ᾽ ἐξοχήν (respecting distinction) it assumes the nature of a proper name; *i. e.*, Satan, ὁ διάβολος, the devil."—Ges. Heb. Lex., Smith's Bib. Dic., vol. 4, p. 2846. Satan is not a translation, but only a Hebrew word put into English. In the New Testament Satan is used, being put into Greek, thirty-five times, in every one of which, excepting two, it designates the arch-fiend.* Διάβολος—in English letters, *Diábolus*—also occurs thirty-five times in the New Testament. In thirty-four of the thirty-five it is the name of Satan. The exception of the thirty-five is when, owing to his unregenerate state, after his call as one of the twelve, he

---

*The exceptions are Matt. 16: 23; Mark. 8: 33. He does not apply the term to Peter, to call him the devil or to imply he was not a child of God. See Smith's Bib. Dic., vol. 4, p. 2846. Like the other disciples, as was the Jewish conception and hope for the Messiah, Peter, believing that Jesus would soon break the Roman yoke and set up an earthly kingdom, eclipsing the brightest days of Solomon's reign, could not think of Jesus being crucified. Yet, as to not have been crucified would have missed the design of Christ's coming into the world and have left it no hope, Peter's protest against it rendered him an adversary—a satan. Just as, through error of understanding, the best people are, in some things, satans—adversaries to the truth. Our version should not here spell satan with a capital.

is called "a devil."—John 6: 70. In the New Testament the devil is, also, six times called Βεελζεβούλ—put into English letters, Beelzeboúl instead of Beelzebub, as our English versions erroneously have it.

*The name Satan describes the arch fiend as the adversary to all good, Beelzebul as the false god, and Diábolus as the "accuser" of the Christian.—Rev. 12: 10. See the lexicons for definitions of the names of Satan.

(2) Demons. Δαιμόνιον and δαίμων—in English letters, *daimónion* and *dáimōn*—are the words for demons. In the Septuagint (the translation of the Old Testament into Greek, made about 280 years B. C.) *daimōnion* and *dáimōn* do not often occur. They are there generally used to speak of heathen gods. The word devil occurs but four times in the Old Testament. It is used twice to render the Hebrew שָׂעִיר—in English letters, *sair*.—Lev.

---

*The New Testament Beelzebub is the Old Testament בַּעַל זְבוּב; in English, spelled *Báal-Zebub*. From Báal, meaning a god, and Zebub, meaning a fly, the word means fly-god—god of the flies—and was worshiped by the Philistines at Ekron, 2 Kings 1: 2. According to the best MSS. the Jews changed it from Zebub to Zebul. Why the change no one knows; probably as a witty ridicule. It came to designate the devil, probably, because he is the sinners' idol.

17: 7 ; 2 Chron. 11: 15. It means a "hairy he goat" which was an object of worship among the Egyptians and the Hebrews, in their idolatrous period. See Ges. Heb. Lex. The other Hebrew word, for "devils," is שֵׁד; in English letters, *shed*. It meant an idol. Gesenius says: "In the Septuagint it occurs in Deut. 32: 17 ; Psa. 106. 37, and the Vulgate renders δαιμόνια *daemonia*, demons, since the Jews regarded idols as demons, which let themselves to be worshiped of men."—Lex. Heb.

Of the use of *daimónion* and *dáimōn*, in Greek literature, Smith's Bib. Dictionary says: "In Homer, where the gods are but supernatural men, it is used interchangeably with Θεὸς (in English letters, *theos*); afterwards, in Hesiod, when the idea of the gods had become more exalted and less familiar, the δαίμονες are spoken of as intermediate beings, the messengers of the gods to men. This later use of the word evidently prevailed afterwards as the correct one. . . . The notion of *evil* demons appears to have belonged to a later period. . . . In Josephus we find the word used always of evil spirits."—Vol. 1, p. 583. From its use by Josephus we see that, in the time of Christ, as seen in the New Testament, *daimónion* and *dáimōn* had come to mean evil spirits. To the increase of light is probably due this change in the use of the words.

To the original use of *daimónion* and *dáimōn* for idols, and to demons being enthroned in the unregenerate heart, is probably in part due their being used for the devils' angels, in New Testament times.

By rendering *diábolus* and *daimónion* and *dáimōn* devils instead of devil and demons, our version has deprived the English reader of the distinction between "the devil and his angels." Matt. 25: 41.

(3) The power, the knowledge and the wisdom of Satan. The great power of any angel, and especially that of an archangel, in view of the expression, "the devil and his angels" (Matt. 25: 41), showing that Satan must have been over the demons when angels, lead us to conclude that Satan has very great power. Alluding, probably, to Satan's power, we read. " But Michael, the archangel, when contending with the devil he disputed about the body of Moses, durst not bring against him a railing judgment, but said, The Lord rebuke thee."— Jude 9. Here Michael, the chief of angels— the archangel—and Satan, the chief of fallen

angels, meet in contention. The passage does not teach that the prince of unfallen angels was afraid of the "prince of the power of the air"— (Eph. 2: 2)—the prince of evil spirits, but, in showing that he was a foe, "worthy of the steel" of the archangel of unfallen angels, appears the power of the devil. Only the archangel was regarded as able to meet the arch-fiend.

In Satan being the archangel of the fallen angels—"the devil and his angels—"he doubtless appears in the rank he had when unfallen; as there is but one archangel in heaven, Satan must have been that archangel. Consequently, Michael, now contending against Satan, was, before the fall, under Satan's command, but now fills the position which Satan filled when in heaven. So the Scriptures speak of "the power of Satan" (Acts 26: 18; 1 Cor. 15: 24; Eph. 2: 2; Col. 1: 13; 2 Thess. 2: 9; Heb. 2: 14) as being very great. Rhetorically, Satan is spoken of as working with "all power"— "the working of Satan with *all* power."— 2 Thess. 2: 9. "Rhetorically," I say; for any one who understands the Scriptures well knows that in the full or literal sense only God has all power.

I now notice the power of a demon. From the power of an unfallen angel we conclude that the power of a demon—a fallen angel—is very great. In Daniel 10: 13 we read that one of these fallen angels withstood an unfallen one "twenty-one" years—a day in prophetic language means year—and could not pass until Michael came to his help.

As to the knowledge and the wisdom of Satan and his angels, when we consider the knowledge and the wisdom of an unfallen angel, and that Satan is thousands of years, and, may be, millions of years, advanced in study and experience, we can but conclude that Satan and his angels, in knowledge and experience, are far beyond the possibility of the utmost stretch of human imagination. By his power and wisdom "Satan fashioneth himself into an angel of light."—2 Cor. 11: 14.

In doing this, Satan seems to sometimes appear in bodily form.* As only the humanity of Christ was the subject of temptation in the wilderness, in that He repelled Satan and called him Satan only in His last of the three temptations, we see that Satan manifested his great power

---

*If any spirits appear in Spiritists' "seances," at the calls of "mediums," here we have a sufficient explanation.

in so fashioning himself as an "angel of light" as to keep Christ ignorant of his true character up to the self-evidently evil nature of his third temptation.* Commenting on Luke 3: 23, Bengel says: "On the other hand, there is also seen, *at times*, from the kingdom of darkness, *bodily appearances.*"

As to the depravity and the positive wickedness of Satan and his angels, in view of their

---

*"Προσελθὼν Αὐτῷ, having come to Him, in a visible form . . . who did not wish it to be known that he was Satan; yet Christ, at the conclusion of the interview, and not till then, calls him, in verse 10, Satan, after that Satan had plainly betrayed his satanity. . . . The tempter seems to have appeared under the form of a γραμματεύς, *scribe*, since our Lord thrice replies to him by the word γεγραπται, it is written."—Bengel on Matt. 4: 3.

In his Commentary, Scott, also, interprets Satan's appearance in bodily form. In view of unfallen angels having appeared in bodily form, it is but to be expected of some of the appearances of the fallen angels. Those who deny that Jesus did not at first recognize Satan, overlook that only his humanity was tempted, and that Satan appears as an angel of light. "Satan gathers all his might and greatness for one more last and decisive onset; but the result is that he hears more decisively and openly pronounced that which befitted his own character. . . . Probably the tempter drew near the first time in human form, as a *good friend* and adviser, . . but now the god of this world comes forward in his naked grossness, with the horrible and undisguised demand, Worship me."—Stier's Words of Jesus, vol. I, pp. 43, 44.

Satan hates to see this.

many thousands of years' sinning, if the brief moment of human life employed in the most outrageous lawlessness renders man unutterably and inconceivably wicked, what must be the "depths of Satan's" and his angels' wickedness!!

As the wickedness of Satan and his angels was noticed in Chapter I., and will further appear in Chapter VI., I will notice that there are, notwithstanding the great wickedness of demons, degrees of wickedness among them—unless, since the Savior was on earth, they have all reached the bottom of wickedness. In Matt. 12: 45, Jesus, speaking of a demon, says: "Then he goeth and taketh with him seven other spirits more evil [$πονηρότερα$—accusative pl. neut. comp.] than himself," on which, commenting, Bengel says: "The seven, however, differ from that one in wickedness, perhaps also among themselves. . . . There are, therefore, unclean spirits who are yet less evil than others; and there are other spirits exceedingly malignant."—*In loco.* So G. W. Clarke's, Barnes' and other commentaries.*

---

*Matt. 12: 43-45, by some, is presumed to speak of demons returning to a regenerate soul and making it again their home. But (1) in that the demon was not "*cast out,*" but went out of *his own will;* (2) instead of the heart being

The number of demons, in Mark 5: 9, is declared "legion." Not taking their own words, which could hardly be doubted, considering their stating their number to Jesus, Luke records, "For many demons had entered into him."—Luke 8: 30. Commenting on Mark 5: 9–13, Bengel says: "If in one nest [dwelling] there can be so many, how many there must be in the whole aggregate throughout the world! . . . The name legion implied a number exceeding this"—exceeding 2,000. Taking into consideration that one demon is in every non-Christian, and that in many cases one non-Christian, like Mary Magdalene and

full of the Holy Spirit, as is a regenerate soul, the demon's going out left it "empty, swept and garnished"; (3) it was his own house while he was away; (4) he was therefore free to invite his companions home with him; (5) had the man, "by grace," been made the temple of God and filled by the Holy Spirit (1 Cor. 3: 16), the demon would not have returned. Prof. McGarvey, perhaps, the ablest Campbellite scholar, says of this passage; "The entrance of such a spirit into a man implied nothing as to his character, and its departure left his character unchanged. . . . The spirit had a kind of a home in it. . . . Finally, it is asked, does the parable teach apostasy? No."—*Apostolic Guide*, January 6, 1888. Stier: "It is not the beginning of regeneration here spoken of, . . . but it is the offense of the hypocrite in false security."—*Words of Jesus*, vol. 2, p. 177.

Satan's work.

the man who dwelt in the tombs, had more than one—some having a great number—the number of demons filling the air very greatly exceeds the number of human beings on the earth. Think of the power, the wisdom, the wickedness and the number of these foul spirits which constitute what God calls "the power of the air."—Eph. 2: 2.

How Satan makes little girls look unlovely.—Eccl. 7: 9; Col. 3: 8.

# CHAPTER V.
## SATAN'S KINGDOM.

By Scott's, Adam Clarke's, Bengel's and other commentaries, and Smith's Bible Dictionary (vol. 4, p. 2848), εἰς ἐμπέσῃ τοῦ διαβόλου—rendered, "fall into the condemnation of the devil" (1 Tim. 3:6)—is understood so as to state that pride was the cause of Satan's fall.

Milton so understands Satan's fall:

> " . . . His pride
> Had cast him out from heaven, with all his host of rebel angels."

And again:

> " My choice
> To reign is worth ambition though in hell."

Milton thus describes Satan's appeal in stirring up war in heaven:

> "Will ye submit your necks and choose to bend
> The supple knee? Ye will not, if I trust
> To know ye right, as if ye know yourselves
> Natives and sons of heaven."

Martensen conjectures that Satan was "Christ's younger brother" (this could have been so only

Father pleading with the boy to not be led by Satan into bad company.—Prov 1: 10; 2: 1-9; 3: 1-6; 4: 13, 14, 15.

by adoption), and "that he became God's adversary because he was not content to be second, but wanted to be first; because he was unwilling to bear the light of another, and wanted to be the light itself." Jacob Böhme : "Lucifer envied the Son his glory; his own beauty deceived him, and he wanted to place himself on the throne of the Son."

While the interpretation, making "Lucifer," mentioned in Isa. 14: 12, mean Satan, which has been extensively received from Jerome, of the fourth century, to the present, is now, by perhaps near all the best interpreters, rejected, yet, that the passage has not a distant allusion to his fall and to pride as its cause, I deem very far from certain. Probably because pride had been Satan's own downfall he resorted to it as best adapted to tempt our first parents and our blessed Savior. However strong this presumption may be, that human experience proves Paul did not err when (1 Tim. 3: 6) he provided against pride as one of Satan's most effective snares, is certainly true.

That there is a vast interval of time between the two first verses of the first chapter of Genesis—maybe many millions of years — is now the understanding of the best interpreters.

Kurtz, and other eminent scholars, hold that the chaotic condition of the world, mentioned in Gen. 1: 2, was the work of Satan—after its creation, in verse 1. In that the Scriptures make the chaotic condition of the world—mentioned in Gen. 1: 2—a type of Satan's work, seen in the chaotic condition of the lost soul—which is implied in being "created in Christ Jesus" (2 Cor. 5: 17; Gal. 6: 15; Eph. 2: 10; 4: 24)—this view seems to have support. But, be this as it may, being cast from heaven into this earth Satan has made it his kingdom.

1. *The Scriptures represent this world as Satan's kingdom.* That Satan and his angels were cast from heaven into this earth, in Chapter II., we saw is the plain teaching of the Bible. Having been cast here, by usurpery, Satan here set up a kingdom for himself. The following Scriptures very plainly speak of Satan as having this world for his kingdom. "If Satan casteth out Satan, he is divided against himself; how then shall his kingdom stand?"—Matt. 12: 26. "How shall the prince of this world be cast out?"—John 12: 31. "The prince of this world cometh."—John 14: 30. "The prince of this world hath been judged."—John 16: 11. "The prince of the power of the air."—Eph. 2: 2. Ἄρχων,

translated "prince," means "one invested with power and dignity, a person of rank and influence, chief ruler, lord." See Grimm's, Cremer's—all the lexicons. Alluding to Satan's rule, broken by Jesus: "Then cometh the end, when he shall have abolished all rule and all authority and power."—1 Cor. 15: 24. These Scriptures not being considered has led preachers to say, "When Satan promised Christ the whole world, if he would worship him, he promised what he possessed not a foot of." But, by usurpery, being king of this world and knowing that Jesus had come to reclaim it, Satan's promise involved this, namely: "As you have come to suffer and die, to wrest my kingdom back into the hands of its true Owner, you fall down and worship me and I will return it without your suffering and death to reclaim it."

2. *How Satan rules.* In Matt. 12: 25 ; 43: 44, 45 ; Eph. 2: 2 ; Matt. 7: 22 ; 8: 16, 31 ; 9: 33; 10: 1, 8 ; 12: 24, 26, 28 ; 17: 19 ; Mark 1: 34 ; 3: 15, 23 ; 16: 9, 17 ; Acts 16: 16 ; 5: 16 ; 8: 7 ; 1 Tim. 4: 1, demons are said to be in unregenerate souls; Matt. 12: 43, 44, 45, and Eph. 2: 2 clearly teaching that they—at least one demon in every son "of disobedience" or unsaved person—dwell or make the soul of

every one who is not a Christian their "house."* Within the Bible is not so much as an intimation that the devil and his angels do not dwell within unsaved sinners in all ages, just as when our blessed Savior was on earth. The above Scriptures, with many others, teach that the works of the devil will be continued on earth until Jesus, at the close of this world's history, "shall have abolished all rule and all authority."—1 Cor. 15: 24. Or, again, as Jesus† teaches, until "the devil and his angels" shall have been "cast into the eternal fire, prepared for the devil and his angels" (Matt. 25: 41), his work in the soul will continue. Satan and his demons residing within the hearts of sinners constitutes their hearts the throne of darkness.

3. *The organization of Satan's kingdom.* In Chapter IV. we have seen that the "kingdom of darkness" is ruled by the devil and demons, the devil being the "prince of demons" (Matt. 12: 24), the demons being called the "angels" of "the devil."—Matt. 25: 41. As the angels of heaven are assigned various offices and mis-

---

\* See Stier's Words of Jesus, vol. 2, p. 176, *et al.*

† Inasmuch as Jesus inspired the apostolic writings, they are as really His words as are His recorded sayings in the Gospels. I have no patience, therefore, with making the Gospels more authoritative than the Epistles.

sions, so are the "angels" of the devil. Angel is not an English word, not a translation, but only an anglicising of the Greek *Άγγελος*, meaning messenger. See the lexicons. Satan, in organizing his kingdom, has at least one demon to every man; several appointed to a work where he deems one insufficient. In the government of nations Satan appoints one demon to the rule of each nation, with, doubtless, a host under that sub-ruler and they distributed as he, under Satan's advice, may deem best. Thus, in Daniel 10: 13, we read of one of these demons having the rule of Persia—"the prince of the kingdom of Persia." In Daniel 10: 20 we read of another demon to whose charge Satan had assigned "Greece"—"the prince of Greece."*

---

* Offering nothing worthy of mention in support of his view, Adam Clarke contents himself with rejecting the view here presented, and interpreting the expression to mean earthly rulers. (1) The narrative bears *prima-facie* evidence in favor of these being some evil supernatural spirits. (2) As well say that "Michael" and the angel who came to Daniel were not angels as to say these were not evil angels. The late Prof. Ezra Abbott, of Harvard University, says: "The prince of Persia, prince of Grecia, and Michael, your prince, are apparently the guardian angels of the nations referred to."—Smith's Bib. Dic., Vol. III., p. 2587 Michael, of God; the others, of Satan. See Gesenius, Rosenmuller, Hitzig, Eisenmenger, *et al.*

This may parallel and explain the devil's deceiving the nations, mentioned in Rev. 20: 3.

Infidelity has objected: "Your having the devil at work all over the world makes him omnipresent."

But, remembering, as we have seen, in Chapter IV., that the demons, under Satan, outnumber earth's inhabitants; that their power over nature is like to that of angels; and that, as with angels, time and space are as nothing, this objection is groundless. A ruler of a great nation, through electricity, has immediate communication with all his government officials throughout his dominion. If necessary, in a few hours, a ruler of a great country can be in any part of his dominion. Considering Satan's power, the power of mind over matter, and that spirits are not subject to matter, to time or to space, how much more easily can Satan be sufficently present to rule the world! Satan's rule, therefore, does not imply omnipresence, but only that he be in close communication with his angels and have power to pass with sufficient swiftness from one part of the globe to the other so as to be, in *effect*, simultaneously present throughout its boundaries. With the wisdom of angels Satan has organized his kingdom—

infinitely more effective than is the organization of Jesuitism.

Not only has Satan thus organized his angels; but, in giving them charge of wicked men and women, he has all sinners organized into his kingdom—just as God has organized Christians into His kingdom.

Trusting this brief and imperfect sketch of the organization of Satan's kingdom will enable the reader to have such a conception of the soul's struggle against the powers of darkness as to feel,

> " My soul, be on thy guard,
> Ten *thousand* foes arise,
> The *hosts* of sin are pressing hard
> To draw thee from the skies,"

I close this chapter.

Have you on this armor?—Eph. 6: 10-17.

Satan tempting to steal.—Eph. 2: 2, 3.

## CHAPTER VI.

### THE WORKS OF SATAN.

1. *Satan the "father" of sin in man.* In Genesis, the third chapter, we see that Satan introduced sin into the world Our blessed Savior's words, that "the devil . . . was a murderer from the beginning" (John 8: 44), imply Satan as the introducer of sin into the world. So do all those Scriptures which speak of the casting out of Satan, the "prince of this world," and his final subjection as the salvation of the earth.

(1) Satan suggests and puts sin into the heart. "After the sop Satan entered into him."—John 13: 27; Luke 22: 3. "Ananias, why hath Satan filled thy heart to lie to the Holy Ghost and to keep back part of the price of the land."—Acts 5: 3. Satan beguiled Eve; moved David to number the people; persuaded Ahab to go up to Ramath Gilead (1 Chron. 21: 1; 1 Kings 22: 21-23.)

Thus Satan puts wicked thoughts and unbelief, of every form and shade, into minds. Not

Satan produces suicide.—Matt. 27: 5.

(72)

only this, but Satan, by preventing the truth from growing, after it has been planted into the heart, is the father of unbelief, causing men in unbelief, to close their eyes to the truth and rush blindly into self-destruction. In the parable of the sower Satan snatches away the word from the heart. Against the counsel of the Lord, Satan led Ahab to go up into a self-destructive battle. (1 Kings 22: 21, etc.; Mark 4: 15.) To Pharaoh's own destruction in the Red Sea, Satan persuaded him to not believe, and to resist the word of the Lord. God, by His *permissive* providence, for men's wickedness, "sends them strong delusion, that they should believe a lie, that they all might be damned who believed not the truth, but had pleasure in unrighteousness."—Ex. 7th to 15th chapters; 2 Thess. 2: 10, 12. Thus deceived, lost souls, confident of peace, like Pharaoh, madly rush into the vortex of eternal punishment, illustrating the Scripture, "There is a way that seemeth right unto a man, but the end thereof are the ways of death."—Prov. 14: 12.

Deceiving "the nations" (Rev. 20: 3), Satan, from the most obscure citizen to the highest ruler, leads them to vote and make iniquitous laws; leads them to believe their numbers, wealth, and other great material strength, render them invulnerable against all danger; and, to their own ruin, leads them into their ungodly wars. To those who are not blinded by "the god of this world" (2 Cor. 4: 4), this lesson is written in letters of living light. Satan stirs up people to steal, rob, and to commit all depredations. Compare Job 1: 12.

(2) Satan, in working his infernal ruin to souls, works wonders.

In his contest before Pharaoh, in deceiving him, Satan wrought such miracles that Pharaoh was, step by step, led into destruction. (See Chapter VII. and "(c)" for full explanation of Pharaoh's case.) God says, "Whose coming is according to the works of Satan with all power and signs and lying wonders [τέρασι ψεύδους—pseudo signs or miracles], and with all deceit of unrighteousness."—2 Thess. 2: 9, 10. "But the Spirit saith expressly that in later times some shall fall away from the faith*, giving heed to

---

\* (1) A sinner or deceived soul can "fall from grace" —that is, from where grace moves on his heart or can reach him.—Gal. 5: 4. (2) A true Christian blackslides in many cases, but never falls from grace. (3) If one true Christian can fall from grace and be lost, so might all; and thus the plan of salvation might be a failure. (4) Paul argues that if we were saved while sinners from being sinners, "much more then, being justified, shall we be saved."—Rom. 5: 9.

seducing spirits and doctrines of devils."—1 Tim. 4: 1.

In Spiritism and in false miracles we have these Scriptures, by Satan and his demons, fulfilled—in τέραοι ψεύδους—pseudo miracles; yet so much like the genuine as to deceive the most worldly wise men.

(3) In leading men into destruction Satan originates false doctrines, "heresies" and false

---

(5) In regeneration we were saved so as to never "depart" from Jesus.—Jer. 32: 39, 40. (6) The Holy Spirit seals—that is, makes *secure*—every believer.—2 Cor. 1: 22; Eph. 1: 13; 4: 30. (7) God continues the saving work in every regenerate soul to the end.—John 13: 1; Phil. 1: 6; Psa. 138: 8. (8) Once in Christ, the believer "can not" sin as does the world.—1 John 3: 6, 9, 10; 5: 18. (9) Every true Christian *has* "EVERLASTING life."—John 5: 24. (10) Every true Christian "shall NEVER perish."—John 10: 28. (11) "All things work together" for the good of the true Christian, instead of any for His falling from grace.—Rom. 8: 28. (12) Jesus prays for all true Christians and by his prayer so anticipates their falls that their faith never fails. His prayer is *always heard*. Compare Luke 22: 32; Heb. 7: 25; John 11: 42. (13) No temptation—nothing—"shall be able to separate us from the love of God which is in Christ Jesus."—Rom. 8: 38, 39; Song of Solomon 8: 6, 7. (14) The Lord will not suffer any child of His to be tempted so as to lead it to fall away from grace.—1 Cor. 10: 13; 2 Peter 2: 9; Job 1: 12; 2: 6, 7. (15) No power can "pluck" a child of God out of God's "hand."—John 10: 28, 29. (16) Temptation, instead of causing the child of God to be lost, only refines

Satan and the bloody knife.—John 8: 44.

churches. Instead of heresies, false doctrines and false churches being tolerated in the Scriptures as mere intellectual infirmities, the Scriptures most severely condemn them. "Now the works of the flesh" (Satan working through the "flesh") . . . "are these, fornication, uncleanness, lasciviousness, idolatry, sorcery" (Spiritism), "enmities, strife, jealousies, wraths, *factions, divisions, heresies*, drunkenness, revel-

him.—1 Peter 1: 7. (17) Instead of falling from grace, the true Christian will come off, not barely saved, barely conqueror, but "*more* than a conqueror."—Rom. 8: 37. All who are *supposed* to have fallen away were only Christians in *profession*. Thus (1), the branch taken away from the vine is only the *sucker* branch.—John 15: 2. (2) The Bible likens one who "falls away" to the "dog" returning "to his vomit," because never a clean animal, and to the "sow" returning to her "wallow," because never a sheep.—2 Peter 2: 22; Prov. 26: 11. Such were Alexander, Hymeneus, Judas, Simon Magus. Thus, Judas is called a devil one year before he betrayed Christ.—John 6: 70. Before the betrayal he is called a thief.—John 12: 6. See Tholuck, *in loco*. So the Scriptures warn us against many professors as false. — Matt. 7: 21-23. John says that instead of the true Christian living as the sinner, "he that committeth sin is of the devil."—1 John 3: 8; and every one who professes to *have* been born of God and yet lives as the world (the Greek is ἔγνωκα—perfect tense, "conveying the double notion of an action terminated in past time and of its effect existing in the present."—Bagster's Lex.) "is a liar."—1 John 2: 4. He tells us that instead of one's life proving falling away, that "in this"—in life, contin-

The poor boy whom Satan led to run off from home.

ings" (χῶμοι, rendered "revelings," Hedericus defines, *saltationes in comessationibus, et saltationes universal*—dancings in merry-makings and dancings in general." So do Liddell and Scott's Lexicon define the word. "Reveling" is here used by the translators as in Byron's poem—"There was a sound of revelry by night"—*i. e.*, sound of dancing. Thus God's word puts dancing in the blackest catalogue of sins.)—Gal. 5: 20, 21. We, therefore, read of "the doctrine

---

uance—"the children of God are manifest and the children of the devil.'—1 John 3: 10. Jesus says that instead of a professor going back proving falling away, "*If* ye *continue* in my word, then are ye *my* disciples."—John 8: 31. So, John says of those whom brethren who believe in "falling from grace," would say had "fallen from grace," "they went out from us, but they were *not of us;* for if they had been of us, they would *no doubt* have *continued* with us."—1 John 2: 19. Such are deliberate hypocrites or the rocky-ground hearers of Luke 8: 13. Not one of the lost professors, at the judgment, had ever by Christ been known as His—not fallen from grace—but Jesus says to them, "I *never* knew you."—Matt. 7: 23. Paul's fear of being "a cast away" had no allusion to fear of being lost, but to fear of not winning the crown—a fear, lest having urged "others" to run the best race, he would be excelled. Compare Dan. 12: 3; 1 Cor. 3: 12-15; 15: 41; Matt. 20: 16. Heb. 6: 4-6, does not mean the true Christian, but rocky-ground hearers, of Luke 8: 13, who never had "root." Num. 22d, 23d and 24th chapters, especially chap. 22: 18; 23: 5-10; 24: 2, 10-13, 16, show that the

Satan in the bad boy.

of Balaam," "the doctrine of the Nicolaitanes," "doctrines of men," and these all being the inspirations of demons, the Scriptures sum them up in the expression, " doctrines of devils," and they exhort us to "sound doctrine." Compare Rev. 2: 14, 15 ; Col. 2: 2, 8 ; 1 Tim. 4: 1-3 ; 1: 19-20 ; 2: 13, 14 ; Tit. 1: 9; 2: 1. Against false doctrines God says: " I testify unto every man that heareth the words of the prophecy of this book, If any man shall add unto them,

---

heathen priest, who never was regenerated, had all that Heb. 6 mentions. The term " sanctified," mentioned in Heb. 10: 29, does not refer to man, but to Christ, as by his " blood " sanctified, *i. e.*, set apart as our Savior—" whom the Father hath sanctified and sent into the world."—John 10: 36. See Scott's Com., *in loco*. A comparison of Ex. 23: 8 ; Deut. 25: 1; 1 Kings 8: 31, 32; Deut. 16: 19, 20; 2 Kings 14: 6, clearly shows that the "righteousness" which is lost, in Ezek. 18: 24, 25 ; 33: 12-16, is not Christ's, but the legal righteousness of the Old Testament. As to angels and our first parents falling, since they never had the "*grace*" of the cross to fall from, were never in the hand of Christ to be "*kept* by the POWER OF GOD, through faith unto salvation" (John 10: 28, 29; 1 Peter 1: 5), but stood only in their own strength and righteousness—being wholly unlike the case of the true Christian—they have no bearing on the question. Since the "love of Christ constraineth," (2 Cor. 5: 14) the Christian to live right, and not the fear of hell, and since all *true* obedience is from *love*, the doctrine of Christ's *preserving* love to the believer will so draw out his heart into His service as to make the *best possible life*.

God shall add unto him the plagues which are written in this book; and if any man shall take away from the words of the book of this prophecy, God shall take away his part from the tree of life, and out of the holy city, which are written in this book."—Rev. 22: 18, 19. Against the devil the Scripture exhorts all who hold the truth to hold "fast the faithful word as he hath been taught, that he may be able by *sound* DOCTRINE both to exhort and to convince gainsayers," and to "speak thou the things which become *sound doctrine.*"—Tit. 1: 9; 2: 1; 2 Tim. 4: 2.\*

(4) Satan's work on the body. Until man admitted Satan into his life, as to *man*, there was neither disease nor death.

(*a*) Producing the death of the body. But when man sinned, according to God's mandate, "in the day that thou eatest thereof thou shalt die" (יָמוּת מוֹת is rendered in Gesenius' Lexicon, "dying, thou shalt die." That is, in both soul and body, dying creatures).—Gen. 2: 17.

---

\* (*a*) Such is the devil's influence on people of these "*last*" times that we find prophecy fulfilled, in their hatred to "doctrine" and to "doctrinal" preaching—even church-members and some ministers thus helping the devil—"For the time will come when they will not *endure* sound doctrine."—2 Tim. 4: 3.

"Sin and death are indissolubly associated together in the Old and the New Testaments. Death is not merely the natural fruit of sin (Jas. 1: 15), but its just punishment as wages (Gen. 2: 17; Rom. 6: 23), and an expression of the divine wrath (Psa. 90: 7-10; Rom. 2: 5-8). We are subject to it because we are subject to the law of sin, and in virtue of our union with Adam (Rom. 5. 17; 1 Cor. 15: 22). It has been denied by some (Pelagius, the Socinians, etc.) that physical death was included in this penalty. The body is regarded as having been mortal before the fall. This view is in contradiction to what seems to be the plain meaning of the words, 'in the day thou eatest thereof thou shalt surely die (*i. e.*, begin to die or become mortal—Gen. 2: 17), when read in the light of the *curse*, in Gen. 3: 19, 'Unto dust shalt thou return.' Although our first parents did not actually return to dust the very day they sinned, nevertheless the principle of death then began to work in them (Augustine, *De Pecc Mer.*, i. 21). Nor is it necessarily true that the body is mortal, especially when we consider its union with the soul. Man was created in the image of God and this might have kept him from the fate of brutes (Dorners' Thelogy ; Oehler,

Satan has taken mother to the grave — Rom. 5: 12.

Theol. of the O. T., sec. 39). This physical immortality was, however, conditional upon his maintaining the state of innocency." (Schaff-Herzog Encyc., vol. 1, p. 618.)

Tholuck: " θάνατος (rendered death) comprehends bodily death, existence in the realm of spirits, the full sense of guilt and misery, each of which is also involved in the other. . . . Where sin exists there the θάνατος (death) appears in all its multifarious modifications, and the consequences which it entails. Even the text, Gen. 2: 17, is applied by the Rabbins to death, in its most comprehensive import.—*in l.* So Crysostom, Theophylact, Grotius, Limborch, Bengel, Schmid, Michaelis, Adam Clarke, Matthew Henry, *et mul. al.* See, also, 1 Cor. 15, especially verses 22, 26, 56.

Satan, by having entered into men's lives and thus bringing death, in the Scriptures, is said to have "the *power* of death."—Heb. 2: 14. Whenever, therefore, we stand and behold the awful and heart-rending scene of our loved ones dying, stand beside their fallen tabernacle, walk through the city of the dead, look upon the crape being worn, hear the wail of the bereaved and behold the widow and the orphan, we see what the "power" of the devil hath wrought.

The old serpent and the fool.—Prov. 23: 32; Rev. 20: 2; Gen. 3: 1.

Yet, sinners will not leave his service for the Giver of life!*

(*b*) Satan producing disease. Disease causing death and Satan's having the "power of death" (Heb. 2: 14) imply that he has the power of producing the cause—disease, in most cases—of death. How any one, accepting the teaching of the Scriptures, that Satan has the "power of death," can doubt that he, therefore, has the "power" of disease is beyond conjecture. (See farther on as to the effect of the fall on nature, under "(*c*)" of this chapter.)

In Chapter I.—as through the whole of this book—that demons are real and personal evil spirits was demonstrated. The position that demonical possessions are but "superstitious notions" finds no favor in the word of God. "The superstition in things of far less moment was denounced by our Lord; can it be supported that He would sanction, and the Evangelists be permitted to record forever, an idea of itself false, which has constantly been the very stronghold of superstition? Nor was the

---

*Because geological history shows that the death of lower animals existed long before man's creation, as if man and they were the same in nature, being and destiny, some have concluded man's physical death not due to the fall.

language used such as can be paralleled with mere conventional expression. 'There is no harm in our speaking of certain forms of madness as lunacy, not thereby implying that we believe the moon to have or to have had any influence upon them; . . . but if we began to describe the cure of such as the moon's ceasing to afflict them, or if a physician were to solemnly address the moon, bidding it abstain from injuring his patient, there would be here a passing over to quite a different region . . . there would be that gulf between our thoughts and words in which the essence of a lie consists. Now Christ does everywhere speak such language as this.' (Trench on Miracles, p. 153, where the whole question is ably treated.) Nor is there, in the whole of the New Testament, the least indication of any 'economy' of teaching on account of the 'hardness' of the Jews' 'hearts.' Possession and its cure are recorded plainly and simply; demoniacs are frequently distinguished from those afflicted with bodily sickness (see Mark 1: 32; 16: 17, 18; Luke 6: 17, 18), even, it would seem, from the epileptic ($\sigma\varepsilon\lambda\eta\nu\iota\alpha\zeta o\mu\varepsilon\nu o\upsilon\varsigma$—subject to epilepsy, Matt. 4: 24); the same outward signs are sometimes referred to possession, sometimes merely to disease (comp. Matt. 4: 24, with 17: 18; Matt. 9: 32, with Mark 7: 32, etc.); the demons are represented as speaking in their own persons with superhuman knowledge, and acknowledging our Lord to be, not, as the Jews generally called him, son of David, but Son of God. (Matt. 8: 29; Mark 1: 24; 5: 7; Luke 4: 41, etc.) All these things speak of a personal power of evil, and if in any case they refer to what we might call mere disease, they, at any rate, tell us of something in it more than a morbid state of bodily organs or self-caused derangement of mind. Nor does our Lord speak of demons as personal spirits of evil to the multitude alone, but, in his secret conversations with his disciples, declares the means and conditions by which power over them could be exercised. (Matt. 17: 21.) Twice, also, He distinctly connects demoniacal possessions with the power of the Evil One; once in Luke 10: 18, to the seventy disciples, where He speaks of His power and theirs over demoniacs as a 'fall of Satan,' and again in Matt. 12: 26-30, where He was accused of casting out demons through Beelzebub, and instead of giving any hint that the possessed were not really under any direct and personal power of evil, He uses an argument, as to the division of Satan against himself, which, if possession be not real, becomes inconclusive and almost insincere. Lastly, the single fact recorded of the entrance of the demons at Gadara (Mark 5: 10–14) into the herd of swine, and the effect which that entrance caused, is sufficient to overthrow the notion that our Lord and the Evangelists do not assert or imply any objective reality of possession."—Smith's Bib. Dic., vol. 1, pp. 585, 586, 587.

Thus, Stier says: "We do not read that the man or the men rushed upon the two thousand swine, to drive them into the sea: it is only said, that the devils went out and entered into them."—Words of Jesus, vol. 1, p. 359. Neander recognizes the absurdity of the demoniac being let loose upon the swine. See Ebrard, in Schaff-Herzog Encyc., vol. 1, p. 624.

From the Scriptures, therefore, that disease and insanity are the works of Satan and his demons is very evident. The insane, in our asylums, in the time our Savior lived on earth would have been called demoniacs. The demoniac, who abode "in the tombs" (Mark 5: 1-12), by any court would now readily be sent to the insane asylum.

*(c) Satan's reign in all physical and animal nature—the fall affecting the whole earth. Genesis 3: 14-20, clearly teaches that by the fall Satan has affected the physical and the animal as well as the spiritual world. The promised "new heaven" and the "new earth" and the making of "all things" new inevitably imply that the fall has wrought direful effect upon the "whole creation."—Rev. 21: 1, 5. God says that, as the effect of the fall, "the *whole creation* groan-

---

\* The cases of the man who was "born blind" (John 9: 32) and the one who "from a *child*" (Mark 9: 14-26) was possessed of "an unclean spirit," show that these unusually badly afflicted cases do not result from any moral offence of their own; but that they come from inheriting the state of fallen humanity. See Psa. 51: 5; Psa. 58: 3; John 3: 6; Eph. 2: 3—Scaff-Herzog Encyclopedia, vol. 1, p. 624; Job 14: 1-4; 11: 12. While not inheriting guilt, inheriting sinful *nature*, as the reader will, from the Scripture just referred to, clearly see, infants inherit all the conditions of disease and death. Dying in infancy, they are not taken to God as they are, but, as Jesus takes them to Himself with one hand, with the other He dips them into His blood, washing from their nature all the effects of the fall. Thus, they enter paradise, not to grow up sinners, but angels. In a late work, called the "Oldest Church Manual," Dr. Philip Schaff, Presbyterian, and the most prominent church historian of America, says: "The Baptists and the Quakers were the first organized Christian communities which detached salvation from ecclesiastical ordinances, and taught the salvation of unbaptized infants and unbaptized but believing adults."

eth and travaileth in pain together" under the rule of Satan.—Rom. 8: 22. On this passage, Tholuck: "It is more natural . . . . to refer it to the concord in the fates of nature and of man." Bengel: "*Creaturarum universitatem*" —"the whole aggregate of creatures without exception is intended"—on Rom. 8: 19. So, Harless' Christian Ethics, p. 36; Robinson's and Grimm's Lexicons on *Κτίσις*; Œcumenius, Ambrose, Matthew Henry, the late Prof. A. N. Arnold in Baptist Quarterly, April, 1867, and a host of interpreters.

In Eph. 2: 2, by speaking of Satan as "the prince of the power of the air," God indorses the then opinion, of both Jews and heathen, that the air is full of evil and active spirits. While God has not permitted Satan to have unlimited rule over men, the lower animals and inanimate nature, yet, that He has given him rule over them, is certain.

Thus, in Job, first chapter, we learn that God permitted Satan to bring "fire" on the earth, originate a cyclone and incite to robbery. Luther was probably right in attributing the origin of mosquitos and other annoying insects to Satan.*

---

* In the plagues of turning rods into "serpents," turning waters into "blood," and making "frogs," it is recorded

At the close of creation God pronounced all His work *good*. I do not believe, therefore, that any pests, *as pests*, then existed. Whether what are now pests existed in any form or condition, is another question. The discords and antagonisms of nature ; its curses and its sorrows, with man, is the "whole creation" in groans and travail. Speaking of the work of Satan, through the fall, Milton re-echoes Rom. 8 : 20–22 :

> "Thus began
> Outrage from lifeless things, but Discord first,
> Daughter of Sin, among the irrational,
> Death introduced, through fierce antipathy:
> Beast now with beast 'gan war, and fowl with fowl,
> And fish with fish ; to graze the herb all leaving,
> Devoured each other ; nor stood much in awe
> Of man, but fled him, or with countenance grim
> Glared on him passing,   These were from without
> The growing miseries, which Adam saw
> Already in part, though hid in gloomiest shade,
> To sorrow abandoned ; but worse felt within,
> And in a troubled sea of passion tossed."

---

that the magicians "did so with their enchantments." Infidel interpreters and some others have explained that these magicians wrought only seeming miracles. But Franklin Johnson, D.D., well says: "But the Scriptures recognize the possibility of miracles from evil sources, Gen. 3 : 1–5; Deut. 13 : 1–5; 1 Sam. 28: 7–25 ; Matt. 24 : 24 ; Luke 11 : 19; 2 Thess. 2 : 3–12; Rev. 13 : 11–14, and gives us a simple test by which we may determine when they are evidences of the

As, before the fall, all nature was harmony—no discord or antagonisms—all peace and bliss; no unfavorable climate, no disease or death to *man;* what a blessed world would this be without Satan! "When the righteous are in authority the people rejoice: but when the wicked beareth rule, the people mourn."—Prov. 29: 2.

In the Satanic reign, in the disruption and the discord of all creation or nature, is the explanation of disease and death. Redemption, in this world, having redeemed only the soul, explains how the infant and the Christian, as the wicked,

---

divine presence, Deut. 13 : 1–5. The demoniacal possessions of Christ's day may be ranked among these wonders of Satan's kingdom. It is possible, also, that modern Spiritualism must be placed in the same category. . . . . There was but little opportunity for deception. . . . . The king had access to the books containing the secrets of the magicians; and if their works were mere tricks they would hardly have hardened his heart, as they are said to have done. There was no doubt much of jugglery connected with ancient magic; but the evidence almost compels the belief that magic was also connected with evil spiritual influences. This alone will account for the severe legislation of Moses against it, Ex. 22: 18; Deut. 18: 10. Crantz: "Angekoks, of Greenland, acknowledged, after their conversion to Christianity, that much of their conjuring had been nothing but trickery; but in a great  eal of it there had

are subject to the difficulties, the trials of this earthly existence, and to disease and death.

In Satan's being the "prince of the power of the air"—ruling in chaotic nature—we have the explanation of his having the "power of death." (Heb. 2: 14.)

As to the medical treatment of disease—meeting the devil by medicine—that this is necessary, is as reasonable as to use means, within the spiritual sphere, for overcoming the devil—praying God to bless the medicines. That God, in the physical as well as in the spiritual realm, should often bless independently of means, is, in the highest degree, to be ex-

---

been some spiritual influence, which they now abhorred, but could not describe." It is almost the unanimous opinion of historians that the magicians, while ready to deceive, had great confidence in the assistance of spiritual influences and it is difficult to read the account of Elijah's interview with the priests on Mount Carmel without the conviction that they expected signs and wonders from their gods.—1 Kings 18: 19-40. Those powers of evil are mercifully restrained within narrow limits."—Moses and Israel, p. 40. Adam Clarke: "There can be no doubt that real serpents were produced by the magicians."—On Ex. 7: 11. In view of God having made only that which was "good" and the power of Satan, within certain limits, to form life, I submit that the more reasonable view is that of Luther—that the devil makes mosquitos and other pests.

pected. Hence, throughout the history of revealed religion are many well proven cases of disease being removed by prayer. To some of them I rejoice in God to say, I am a personal witness—some in my own case. Of the "presbyters," by anointing with oil, and prayer curing sickness, commenting on Jas. 5: 14, Bengel says: "This was the highest faculty of medicine in the Church." (The anointing was a symbol of the Holy Spirit, by Whom they were healed.) That God is as ready as ever to heal the sick, in answer to the prayer of faith, I have no doubt. In apostolic times it seems, as now, that but few had the gift of healing the sick. Compare Matt. 4: 23; Luke 9: 6; Acts 10: 38; and 1 Cor. 12: 9, 28, 29, where you will see that not all had the "gift of healing." As Paul left Trophimus at Miletus "sick" (2 Tim. 4: 29), it is evident that he had not the "gift of healing"—at least, at all times; *or*, that it was not the Lord's will, in that case, to heal at present Yet—this by the way—I advise no one, unless *very certain of healing faith*, to dispense with medicine. In the next chapter will be noticed why God permits Satan to afflict—especially to afflict infants and Christians.

## CHAPTER VII.

GOD OVERRULING SATAN AND MAKING HIM HIS AGENT FOR THE GREATEST GOOD AND FOR HIS GLORY.

"The Satan of the Scriptures is a portrait independent of Persian mythology. He and Ahriman agree only in this, that they are alike spirits of evil. . . . Ahriman rules over half the world and is independent of Ormuzd. Satan's dominion is limited and subject to the supreme authority of God. Ahriman is co-eternal with Ormuzd, Satan is a creature who apostatized from the truth."—Schaff-Herzog Ency., vol. I, p. 632.

*That God rules all things after the infinite counsel of His own blessed will is the teaching of the Bible.* "For I am God, and there is none else; I am God, and there is none like me; \* de-

---

\* The teaching of some German and Dutch infidels, accepted and aped by certain English and American scholars, because being put forth under the *imprimatur* of "German scholarship," that Jehovah, like the gods of other nations, was but a tutelary or tribal god is ridiculously and wickedly absurd.

Jesus makes a dying bed soft as downy pillows are.—Num. 23: 10.

claring the end from the beginning, and from the ancient times things that are not yet done; saying, My counsel shall stand, and I will do all my pleasure."—Isa. 46: 9, 10.

> "See that I, even I, am he,
> And there is no god with me:
> I kill, and I make alive;
> I have wounded, and I heal:
> And there is none that can deliver out of my hand.
> For I lift up my hand to heaven,
> And say, I live forever.
> If I whet my glittering sword,
> And mine hand take hold on judgment;
> I will render vengeance to mine adversaries,
> And will recompense them that hate me."
> —Deut. 32: 39-41.

"I know there is no God in all the earth [that is, He is the only God] but in Israel."—2 Kings 5: 15. "I am the first, and I am the last; and beside me there is no God."—Isa. 44: 6.

> "The Lord hath established his throne in the heavens;
> And his kingdom ruleth over all."—Psa. 103: 19.

Under the supreme and independent Ruler the Christian triumphantly and joyfully exclaims: "We know that to them that love God, all things work together [$\sigma \upsilon \nu \varepsilon \rho \gamma \varepsilon \tilde{\iota}\ \varepsilon \iota \varsigma\ \dot{\alpha} \gamma \alpha \theta \acute{o} \nu$—literally, work together into good] to them that are called according to his purpose."—Rom. 8: 28.

"For our light affliction, which is for the moment, worketh for us more and more exceedingly an eternal weight of glory."—2 Cor. 4: 17

When Satan and his angels were cast out, into the earth, instead of being given here absolute power, it is recorded that God put them into "chains" or bonds—not literal "chains," but, as Adam Clarke says, "'chains of darkness' is a highly poetic expression"; an expression indicating that God holds Satan in His own power and that Satan's reign, instead of being infinite, is limited by the wisdom, the power and the goodness of Him who worketh all things after the infinite counsel of His own irresistible and blessed will. God, therefore, in all things, so overrules Satan that "all things" he does he only glorifies God, works good to the Christian and "spits into his own face." To illustrate—
(*a*) Christ said to Peter: "Simon, Simon, behold, Satan asked to have you, that he might sift you as wheat: but I have made supplication for thee, that thy faith fail not"—$ἵνα\ μή\ εκλίπῃ\ ἡ\ πίστις\ σου$, literally, that thy faith should not possibly entirely fail thee.*—Luke 22: 32.

---

\* See Cremer's, Grimm's—the Lexicons—on $εκλίπη$. So Stier, Bengel, Matthew Henry, *et al*. It is the 2 Aorist subjunctive—possibility. See Winer's N. T. Gram., p. 287.

Ἐξῃτήσατο, rendered, in the New and the Bible Union Versions, "asked" (though the verb is in the middle voice, it is here used as active, as the middle and the active are sometimes interchangeable—Winer's N. T. Gram., p. 256)—a rendering sustained by the Lexicons and the Commentaries.* The marginal rendering of the New Version is, "obtained you by asking." Paraphrased: "Satan has asked me for you, to destroy you, as he is destroying Judas, who never was a child of God (John 6: 70, 71); I have granted the request, but have so limited it, by my prayer, that your faith, while it will be partly eclipsed (Ἐκλίπῃ, rendered "fail," in Greek classics, says Grimm's Lexicon, means to eclipse, and it is the word whence comes our word "eclipse," which means, not failure or extinction, but covering or hiding), should not be utterly eclipsed; and that, instead of the trial destroying you, it shall be overruled to sifting the chaff and the trash from you and in making you a better Christian." As Lange comments: "The holy supplication of mercy countervails before God the daring appeal of the accuser." And as

---

* Cremer's, Grimm's, Greenfield's, Bagster's, Liddell and Scott's, and Robinson's Lexicons—doubtless, all others. By Commentators Stier, Alford, Bengel, etc.

Stier: "The Father's grace, prayed for by the Son, defends from this ruin" (falling from grace); "and not only so, but the superabundance of His grace makes the experience thus gained of our infirmity and impotence the means of strengthening our faith when we are delivered. Christ did not pray that from the sifting we should be spared; but that we might not through perfect unbelief become chaff which must fall through. The fulfillment of His supplication takes place in that He can strengthen our faith and preserve and revive the spark which was ready to be extinguished, through that prerogative of grace which is of more avail before God than the demand of the accuser."—Words of Jesus, Vol. 7, page 177. Bengel: "Even though Satan sifted Peter, yet he did not altogether wrest from him his faith. Satan sought to cause an eclipse of faith in Peter; but the light of faith immediately shone out again in him after the *strife* [v. 24] and after the subsequent denial."—*in loco*. So, as Providence had arranged to remind Peter of Christ's warning (compare Luke 22: 34 and 62), the "cock" crowed at his denial, and, then, in fulfillment of Christ's prayer, Peter's faith manifested itself in that "he went out and wept bitterly" and was, as an erring child, most tenderly forgiven. From this, in fulfillment of Christ's words: "And do thou, when once thou hast turned again [New Ver.] establish thy brethren."— Luke 22: 32. Peter's faith passed out of the eclipse, and he became a much stronger Christian than before his fall or denial. When, about twenty-seven years after Peter's fall, it became necessary for some one to write to the fiery, being tested Christians, "scattered" abroad by persecution, from his own experience Peter was selected to write that epistle. As they read his words, "For a little while, if need be ye have been put to grief in manifold temptations, that the proof of your faith being much more precious than gold that perisheth, though it be proved by fire, might be found into praise and glory and honor at the revelation of Jesus Christ. . . . Be sober, be watchful: your adversary, the devil, as a roaring lion, walketh about, seeking whom he may devour," I say, as these tempted ones read these words (1 Pet. 1: 5-8; 5:8), how exultingly they exclaimed, Why, to encourage us, Peter is alluding to how his own trial *refined* him, as fire does the gold, and to the *certain* victory of our faith by Christ's prayer for us so *overruling Satan*, that instead of his making us "fall from grace," he will, as he did Peter, but "sift" and make us the more brightly reflect our blessed Savior! Little did Satan dream that his attempt to destroy Peter's faith would be so overruled that it would purify and strengthen it, and make him the means to "establish" (Luke 22: 32) his brethren, by his personal ministry and by his epistles, until the Son of man shall come on "the throne of His glory."

(*b.*) Job's case is a like illustration. The devil, as he "asked" for Peter, asked for Job. (Job 1: 7–12.) God granted the devil's request, saying: "Behold, all that he has is in thy power; only upon himself put not forth thine hand."--Job 1: 12. Under this divine permission, expecting to cause Job to fall from grace,* the devil darkened the life of Job by most trying afflictions. Reading from the first to near the latter part of the Book of Job, the reader, in confusion, feels to exclaim: "Why did God permit such fearful trials to befall His servant Job?" But, in the close of the trial, he reads that Satan, instead of causing Job to fall from grace, brought him to see more of his un-

---

* Satan, as well as some good people, has always believed that God's people may "fall from grace."

worthiness and nearer to God—Job 41:6: "Wherefore I abhor myself, and repent in dust and ashes"—and that "the Lord gave Job twice as much as he had before" (Job 42: 10-17), etc. What a blessed close of trials and of life was Job's! And as we think that Satan, thus sifting Job, has been overruled as a blessing through all time, in being made to solve the enigma of life and, by solving it, has thrown such light into the furnace of life, by which, looking into it, we see Jesus walking there with us, and see ourselves, instead of being therein destroyed, finally coming out without a "singe," and with only our earthly *fetters* (Dan. 3: 25, 27) *burned off*, "guarded . . . . . that the proof of your faith, being much more precious than of gold that perisheth, though it is proved by fire, might be found into praise and glory and honor at the revelation of Jesus Christ" (1 Pet. 1: 5-7, New Ver.), we exclaim rejoicingly:

> "Judge not the Lord by feeble sense,
> But trust Him for His grace;
> Behind a frowning providence
> He hides a smiling face.
> Blind unbelief is sure to err
> And scan His work in vain;
> God is his own interpreter,
> And he will make it plain.

> Ye fearful saints, fresh courage take;
> The clouds ye so much dread
> Are full with grace and will break
> With blessings on your head."

(*c*) Pharaoh's case is another illustration of how God uses Satan. As a judgment on Pharaoh for his wickedness, God said: "I will harden his heart, and he will not let the people go."—Ex. 4: 21. This does not, as some have thought, mean that God made Pharaoh a sinner. Pharaoh was a very wicked man, as is seen in his outrages on the Jews. (Compare Ex. 1: 8-22; 5: 2, 4-19. The Pharaoh of chapter 5 indorsed the one of chapter 1.) For his outrages on the Jews and his *determined* persistency in wickedness, God designed the destruction of his hosts in the Red Sea. To get him to rush his hosts into the sea it was necessary to so "harden" his heart that he would be blinded to all danger. In hardening him, by permiting Satan to work miracles before him and to otherwise influence him, God made Satan His agent. Thus, there being *no hope of repentance* in Pharaoh, God used Satan in so hardening his heart against danger, that he rushed his army into destruction. This is an illustration of 2 Thess. 2: 10, 11:—"And with all deceit of unrighteousness for them that are perishing; *because* they received not the *love of the truth* that they might be saved. And for *this cause God sendeth* them a working of error, that they should believe a lie: that they all might be *judged* who believed not the truth, but had PLEASURE *in unrighteousness"*—and 2 Thess. 2: 10, 11, illustrates Pharaoh's case.

By permitting Satan to pervert the Bible and thereby make it a snare, a delusion—judicial punishment to those who do not have sufficient regard for it to earnestly and honestly study it —God makes him His agent, in accomplishing the very opposite to that He accomplishes, through the Bible, in the case of those who love, earnestly and honestly study it. To this Paul alluded when he said, of the gospel, "to the one a savor from death unto death; to the other a savor from life unto life."—2 Cor. 2: 16.

\* As Harless remarks: "Christ Himself is to the one man the instrument of salvation, to another the instrument of condemnation—to the one 'the savor of life unto life,' to another 'the savor of death unto death'—in one and the

---

\* "Ὀσμη—such an odor as is emitted by death (*i. e.*, by a deadly pestiferous thing, a dead body), and itself causes death."—Grimm's N. T. Lex.

What Satan hates.—Prov. 22: 6.

same testimony bringing forth as well as awakening reproof and condemnation." — Christian Ethics, p. 376. In making the Holy Scriptures, through the Spirit, the means of salvation to those who rightly use them, and to the persistently disobedient, through Satan, making the same Scriptures judicial punishment, what wonderful wisdom and economy! The same thing is true as to affliction. We see God letting Satan, by disease and all kinds of suffering, harden those who, like Pharaoh, are *decided* to never repent, that they the more blindly rush into destruction; while, through the Holy Spirit, we see the same afflictions so sanctified that, with the Psalmist, we experience, "Before I was afflicted I went astray; but now I observe thy word." (Psa. 119: 67.) Thus, while God uses the Spirit in making "all things work together for good to them that are called according to his purpose" (Rom. 8: 28), He uses Satan, by His permissive providence, to make "all things work together" to accomplish His righteous judgment upon the disobedient, so that "even the lamp [Rev. Ver.] of the wicked is sin." (Prov. 21: 4.)

The Crucifixion is another illustration. For the world to be saved, Christ must be crucified.

In Satan's instigating* the crucifiers, his intention to destroy Christ and His kingdom was turned, by the Lord, into the hope of the world and the destruction of the kingdom of darkness. In imprisoning John Bunyan, Satan's attempt at his destruction blessed the world with "Pilgrim's Progress." Satan attempting, through persecution, to destroy the Church, in its early history, under God, so purified it and increased its numbers that Tertullian, living among the early Christians, in triumph, said, *Semen est sanguis Christianorum*—the blood of the martyrs is the seed of the Church—the seed of Christians.

While we can not always see it so, as we are but prattling children, on our Father's knee, doubtless, every move which Satan ever made, now makes and ever will make, has been, is and ever will be so overruled by the Lord, that out of it the very highest and widest good will ultimate.

Who knows how many millions of worlds are inhabited which, by the fearful work which Satan hath wrought on our little globe, are prevented from falling? Without the fall how

---

* Διάβολος, "in the Bible the author of evil, estranging mankind from God and enticing them to sin."—Grimm's N. T. Lex.

could we have had our love for righteousness and for God, by the horror of sin, enhanced? Without the fall furnishing occasion for the infinite manifestation of God's love, in the gift of His Son, how could angels and men have ever realized such blissful contemplation and power of His love? Was it not to this the apostle alluded, when, in rapture, he exclaimed: "Unto me . . . was given to preach unto the Gentiles the *unsearchable riches of Christ;* and to make all men see what is the dispensation of the mystery which from all ages hath been hid in God, who created all things; to the intent that now unto the principalities and the powers in the *heavenly* places\* might be *known* through the Church the manifold wisdom of God, according to the eternal purpose which he purposed in Christ Jesus." (Eph. 3: 8–11, 16; 1: 6; Rom. 9: 23.)

---

\* The passage certainly means the glory of His grace revealed to both men and angels in heaven. Ἐπουρανίοις, Grimm's N. T. Lex, for this passage, defines: "Heaven itself, the abode of God and angels." Ἐξουσιαις Grimm defines, for this passage, "a certain class of angels." So Robinson's N. T. Lex. and Bagster's, on both these words. So McKnight's, Henry's, Scott's, Adam Clarke's Com., Smith's Bib. Dic., vol. 3, p. 2588.

Without Satan effecting the fall, how could the poor blind girl have ever written:

> "Could we with ink the ocean fill,
>   And were the sky of parchment made;
> Were every blade of grass a quill,
>   And every man a scribe by trade—
> To write the love of God with ink
>   Would drain the ocean dry;
> Nor would the scroll contain the whole,
>   Though spread from sky to sky."

Julius Müller says: "It is not usually God's method to display His greatest thoughts ostentatiously, He rather conceals them, quenching their beams from bold and presumptuous eyes, and hiding his higher works beneath a plain and simple form."—Christian Doctrine of Sin, vol. 2, p. 94.

While there are many things God has revealed to us, concerning His overruling Satan and, thus, using him for the accomplishment of His purposes, He has left much to reveal to us in the "ages to come." (Eph. 2: 7.) Until all things are made clear by yet greater light than mortal eyes can bear, from those that have been made clear, we rest satisfied to join Julius Müller in saying: "Apart from us, as the apostle warns us (Rom. 11: 24), God may have secret thoughts over and above those which He makes known to us; thoughts which shall not, peradventure, be fully revealed until His kingdom is far more widely developed, and perhaps not in their fullness even then."—Christian Doctrine of Sin, vol. 2, p. 199.

# CHAPTER VIII.

## THE FINAL TRIUMPH OF CHRIST AND THE END OF SATAN AND HIS KINGDOM.

. . . . . "Now thou hast avenged
Supplanted Adam, and by vanquishing
Temptation, hast regained lost paradise,
And frustrated the conquest fraudulent:
He never more henceforth will dare set foot
In paradise to tempt; his snares are broke:
For though the seat of earthly bliss he failed,
A fairer paradise is founded now
For Adam and his chosen sons, whom thou
A Savior art come down to reinstall
Where they shall dwell secure when time shall be
Of tempter and temptation without fear."
—*Milton's " Paradise Regained."*

"Jesus shall reign where'er the sun
  Doth his successive journeys run;
  His kingdom stretch from shore to shore,
  Till moons shall wax and wane no more.

"Blessings abound where'er he reigns,
  The prisoner leaps to break his chains;
  The weary find eternal rest,
  And all the sons of earth are blest.

Christ delivering from the Captivity of Satan.—2 Tim. 2: 26; Luke 4: 18.

> "Let every creature rise, and bring
> Peculiar honors to our King;
> Angels descend with songs again,
> And earth repeat the loud amen."
>
> —*Isaac Watts.*

1. *Though human poetry, this bright picture is more than fully true;* for "we have the word of prophecy more sure; whereby we do well that we take heed, as unto a lamp shining in a dark place until the day dawn."—2 Pet. 1: 19. "He shall have dominion also from sea to sea, and from* the river unto the ends of the earth." (Psa. 72: 8; read the whole Psalm) "To this end was the Son of God manifested, that he might destroy the works of the devil." (1 John 3: 8.) "Now is the judgment of this world: now shall the prince of this world be cast out." (John 12: 31; 16: 11; νῦν, rendered "now," is here used in the sense of "forthwith."— (Grimm's N. T. Lex.) This is prophetic, putting the future, because of its certainty, as present.

Jesus, by His satisfaction of the violated law of God, which violation, without the satisfaction, prevented God from blessing the world,

---

* In the original much of the Old Testament is poetry, and the finest poetry.

in casting out Satan and in removing, for all who believe on Jesus (John 3: 15, 16; 5: 24; 6: 47; Acts 16: 30, 31, Rom. 4: 5; 5: 1; 3:26). every trace of the curse, destroys "the works of the devil."

This destruction is effected in removing Satan and his angels from the earth and in removing the effects of the fall. "And I saw an angel coming down out of heaven having the key of the abyss and a great chain in his hand. And he laid hold on the dragon, the old serpent, which is the devil and Satan, and bound him a thousand years, and cast him into the abyss,* and shut it up and set a seal over him, that he should deceive the nations no more, until the thousand years should be finished: after this he must be loosed a little season." (Rev. 20: 1–3.)

Satan being shut up, voters, law-making bodies and rulers being no longer misled by him, and God's terrible judgments having broken (Rev. chapter 6 to chapter 20) the pow-

---

* Ἄβυσσον is the word, in the Common Version, in Luke 8: 31, rendered "deep," a very misleading rendering, as it conveys the idea of the sea; whereas, in the sea was where these demons desired to go, as manifest in their entering the swine and through them into the sea. It is not hell, but a place of punishment, till the final sentence—probably one department of *hades*.

God's work, to save from the devil's, as seen in the distressed wife and child.—Prov. 23: 29-32.

ers of wickedness on earth, such as the rum, wine and beer traffic; the Arab African slave trade; the organized licentious and female seducing powers; great and corrupt political parties and nations, etc.; the soil and the climate restored to their primeval (Psa. 72: 16; 67: 5; Ezek. 34: 25-31; Isa. 4: 2 to end of chapter; 29: 17; 32: 15; 65: 21; Zech. 8: 12; Mal. 3: 11) condition, we shall, to a great extent, have Satan and his works destroyed. A comparison of these Scriptures, here in parenthesis referred to, clearly teaches that with Satan's dominion ended, in the language of two of them, then shall " the wilderness become a fruitful field, and the fruitful field become a forest": "I will cause the shower to come down in its season; there shall be showers of blessing. And the tree of the field shall yield its fruit, and the earth shall yield her increase." Though especially intended for Palestine,* these Scriptures are intended to include the whole earth.

With Eden restored and the highest state of scientific cultivation of the soil, the earth giving up her countless secret treasures, hidden

---

* Now, that Christ's coming is near, and the Jews are being restored to Palestine, travelers report that the seasons there are being strangely restored.

from a sinful world until the blessed day, and all business conducted upon the most scientific principles, Texas is capable of sustaining, most comfortably and happily, more than earth's living population, while the United States could probably thus sustain more than the number who have ever lived on the earth. But, as material prosperity increases the prodigality of the prodigal, so the Edenic condition would insure such material prosperity as to lead to such idolatry of the material, and consequent moral and spiritual degradation, as to make this earth much more like hell than it is.

Sir James Thornhill, a famous painter, many years ago, was employed to ornament the roof of St. Paul's Church, in London. On a very high scaffold he was just giving his beautiful work the finishing touches. Entranced with the beauty of his work and forgetting his danger, to better view it, he was stepping back from it, when one of his assistants happened to cast his eye on him. Seeing that another step would dash his life out on the pavement below, and seeing it would not do to speak to him, he dashed the brush over the beautiful picture, spoiling many weeks' labor. Springing forward in astonishment and wrath, Sir James de-

Satan doesn't live here.

manded, "Why this outrage?" to which his faithful assistant answered, "Look down the dizzy heights below us and see where, in one moment more, you would have been dashed had I not done so;" on which he grasped his assistant's hand, threw his arm around him and wept with gratitude. So our God, in great love, pity and solicitude, has used Satan to blot out Edenic beauty, loveliness, comfort and happiness of this world until "the prince of this world" is "cast out." As Sir James Thornhill, without the spoiling of the picture, would have perished, so, even the cross could not have saved men from the dizzy height of this world's Edenic prosperity (as it is, most men are so captivated by the world that they are not drawn to the Savior), had not God rendered it "a wilderness of woe." In eternity, when God, from the dizzy heights of heaven, shall point us to the hell below, and say, Look where you would have been had I left the earth in its primeval glory, we will fall at his feet, embrace and thank Him for the afflictions of earth as much or more than for what, in our blindness, are thought only its blessings.

In the Apocalypse (in our version called "Revelation"), a day is used for a year. With this, multiplying the one thousand, of Rev. 20: 2, by the number of days in a year, we have an Edenic reign of righteousness of three hundred and sixty-five thousand years for this poor earth, in which Christ and His people reign together. Here is the inheritance of "the earth" for "the meek" (Matt. 5: 5), and the heirship and the "joint" heirship of Rom. 8: 17.* Though poor as Lazarus, and singing,

> "Not a foot of land do I possess,
> Nor cottage by the sea,"

dear reader, if a child of God, in destroying "the works of the devil," praise God, Jesus has made you the child of the King—incomparably richer than the richest poor lost one on earth.

Well do I remember when, with the understanding that this earth would continue about seven thousand years and then be "burned up," with great perplexity, I said: "Why did God make the world to continue only a short time, that time being reigned over by Satan, to be burned up?" But, in view of the "sure word of prophecy," that Christ's coming is

---

*Many, thoughtlessly reading of this heirship, imagine it is heaven. Why, dear Christian, Jesus never inherited heaven—it was always His. Consequently, heaven can not be our joint heirship.

near, which will "cast out the" usurping "prince of this world," followed by the three hundred and sixty-five thousand years of the reign of righteousness and of "peace on earth and good will unto men," what consolation and encouragement for all who, against sin and crime, are "battling for the Lord." While other causes and enterprises may fail and other kingdoms crumble into dust, the Christian cause is as certain of final victory and His kingdom to be an "everlasting kingdom" as is the very throne of the Omnipotent.

> "Behold, the mountain of the Lord
>   In latter days shall rise
> Above the mountains and the hills,
>   And draw the wondering eyes."

> "The beam that shines on Zion's hill
>   Shall lighten every land;
> The King who reigns in Zion's towers
>   Shall all the world command.

> "No strife shall vex Messiah's reign,
>   Or mar the peaceful years;
> To ploughshares soon they beat their swords,
>   To pruning-hooks their spears.

> "No longer hosts encountering hosts,
>   Their millions slain deplore;
> They hang the trumpet in the hall,
>   And study war no more."

2. *Though the Christian, to keep Satan from ruling him, is kept in continuous warfare, and though sometimes, for a moment,* **defeated***, yet, by the grace of Jesus, he now has victory over Satan and his demons.*

"I will appear unto thee, delivering thee from the people and from the Gentiles, . . . to open their eyes that they may turn from darkness to light, and from the power of Satan [$τῆς ἐξουσίας τοῦ σατανᾶ$—the power, authority and government of Satan. See Grimm's, Cremer's—all Lexs.] unto God." (Acts 26: 18. "Being made free from sin, ye become the servants of righteousness." (Rom. 6: 18.) "With freedom did Christ set us free." (Gal. 5: 1.) "Giving thanks unto the Father, who made us meet to be partakers of the inheritance of the saints of light; who delivered us out of the power of darkness [$ἐκ τῆς ἐξουσίας τοῦ σκότους$—out of the power, authority and government of darkness.—See the Lexs.] and translated us into the kingdom of the Son of his love." (Col. 1: 12, 13.) By God's unmerited favor ("grace") translated from Satan's kingdom into "the kingdom of the Son of his love," we are, by the same "grace" "guarded, through faith, unto salvation, ready to be revealed in the last day."

(1 Pet. 1: 5.) Φρουρουμένους, spelled in English, *phrouroumenous*, Grimm's Lexicon defines: "To guard, protect by a military guard, either in order to prevent hostile invasion, or to keep inhabitants of a besieged city from flight . . . metaphorically, to protect by guarding."—See the other Lexicons, by which it is also clear that, in rendering it "guarded," the Revised Version is correct. In answer, then, to the question, "How is a poor and weak Christian to withstand the continuous assaults of Satan and his demons?" we are "guarded" by legions of angels, and by the Holy Spirit strengthening and preserving us inwardly and outwardly—"GUARDED"! (See 2 Kings 6: 16, 17; Matt. 18: 10; Heb. 1: 14; 12: 22; Matt. 4: 11. By reading these references the reader will get a rich feast on angelic ministries.) The guarding of God's saints makes it so far beyond the possibility of one of them ever being overthrown and lost that Paul rapturously exclaims: "Who shall separate us from the love of Christ? Shall tribulation, or anguish, or persecution, or famine, or nakedness, or peril, or sword? . . . Nay, in all these things we are more than conquerors *through him that loved us.* For I am persuaded that neither death, nor life, nor

angels, nor principalities, nor things present, nor things to come, nor powers, nor height, nor depth, nor any other creature, shall be able to separate* us from the love of God, which is in [that is, saves us only through Christ] Christ Jesus our Lord." (Rom. 8: 35-39.)

---

*The reply is often made to all this: " Yes, but we can separate ourselves from God and thus fall from grace." But, if the reader will carefully *re*-read the passage, he will see that, by mentioning all the trials and temptations (for only thus, if at all, could we be led to do so), that is just what Paul says *will not be done*. Who would imagine that Paul would make such effort to prove what all know true—that " God will not let us be separated *while faithful!*" We need promises for our weaknesses; not because of our strength, as the " falling from grace " discouragement and uncertain gospel (?) would have it. Beautiful and sweet is the comment on this passage. Tholuck, here, quotes from Theodoret, a Christian writer of the early part of the fifth century: " Having weighed all nature in the scale with love towards God, and having with the things that are seen, connected things known only by the intellect, angels and principalities and powers, and with present blessings, those that are expected in the future, yes, and even the punishments which are threatened and in addition to these, eternal life and eternal death ; and having perceived this part to be as yet defective, he seeks something else to add, and not finding it, fabricates, with a word, *another creation*, equally great and manifold, and not even thus does he see all these things equaling the love of God"—*i. e.*, able to lead from Christ's love.

3. *While preserving us, all disease and afflictions are, by grace, made only chastisements—bringing the Christian nearer to God.*

To the persistently impenitent all suffering is a " consuming fire " (Heb. 12: 29) ; to the Christian all suffering is a refining fire. (1 Pet. 1: 7.) To the former "all things work together" for pouring justice on him ; to the latter "all things work together for good"—mercy and love, even in the severest suffering. (Rom. 8: 28; Heb. 12: 5–11. The reader please here prayerfully read Chapter VII., especially "(*a*)" and "(*b*)" of that chapter, as therein this is explained.)

5. *After all chastisements are over, the Christian will rejoice in the complete salvation and the complete victory over all foes.* In consideration of the Christian being beyond the possibility of ever being lost, the Scriptures speak of him as *now* having everlasting life—as being *now* saved. " Verily, verily, I say unto you, He that . . . . believeth on me HATH EVERLASTING life . . . . and *shall not* come into contemnation." (John 5: 24.) " Verily, verily, I say unto you, He that believeth on me HATH EVERLASTING life." (John 6: 47.) Hence, Acts 2: 47, as rightly rendered, in the Bible

Union Version, reads: "The Lord added to the church daily those who *are* saved."*

Inasmuch as our present salvation is the regeneration of only the soul, and the body is not delivered from Satan, except by the *indirect* work of the soul, in controlling it (see Rom. 8: 13, 23; 1 Cor. 9: 27; Rom. 13: 14; Gal. 5: 17, 24), when the body is regenerated, *i. e.*, when we are raised with the completely redeemed or resurrection body, we have the completion of our salvation--not of the soul, but in destroying Satan's last hold, "the redemption of our bodies." (Rom. 8: 23; 1 Cor. 15: 26, 57; Phil. 3: 21.) Notwithstanding that the soul being "saved" forever is the *pledge* of the salvation

---

*In rendering it "those that were being saved," the English revisers, of the Revised Version, meant " the saved," but rendered it a participle, to mean, were being saved as each one was saved--history of grace then saving. Agreeing in the meaning, but to remove all possible obscurity, the American reviser wanted it rendered "those that were saved." Adam Clarke comments: "Those who were saved . . . in opposition to those who were lost"—*in. l* Hackett: "Already secured their salvation "—*in. l.* Bloomfield: " If we keep close to the *proprietas linguæ* . . . . we can not translate otherwise than 'the saved,' those who were saved, as the expression is rendered by Doddridge and Mr. Wesley, which is supported by the authority of the Pesch. Syr. Ver."--*in. l.* On τοὺς σ_ _μενους being rendered " the saved," see Winer's N. T. Gr_m., p. 353.

of the body, such is the relation of soul and body to the person whom they constitute that the "redemption of the body" is also called "salvation." (Rom. 8: 23; 13: 11; Heb. 1: 14.)

When we shall have received our resurrection bodies, in the completest sense we will realize that the last vestige of Satan's work has been destroyed from our natures. With the new earth, with the bodies that are subject to neither suffering nor death, and with our reunion with those whom the destroyer has in death cut down and separated from us, we will be the fulfillment of the blessed promise: "And I heard a great voice out of the throne saying, Behold, the tabernacle of God is with men, and he shall dwell with them, and they shall be his people, and God himself shall be with them, and be their God: and he shall wipe away every tear from their eyes; and death shall be no more; neither shall there be any mourning, nor crying, nor pain any more: the first things are passed away. And he that sitteth on the throne said, Behold, I make all things new." (Rev. 21: 3-5.)

6. *The final doom of Satan, his angels and all persistently impenitent.*

In 2 Pet. 2: 4, and Jude 6, we learn that when God cast Satan and his angels into this earth

He did not intend it as their final place. That their final doom has not yet come the demons recognized, when they said to Jesus, "Art thou come hither to torment us before the time?" (Matt. 8: 29.) At the final close of the curse we read Satan's and his demons' sentence, and that of all wicked men and women: "Depart, ye cursed, into everlasting fire prepared for the devil and his angels." (Matt. 25: 41.) "This is the second death, even the lake of fire. And if any one was not found written in the book of life, he was cast into the lake of fire." (Rev. 20: 14, 15.) Satan sinning without any one to tempt him there was no Savior for him. An offered Savior is such a blessing that His rejection being as great a sin as sinning without temptation, and there being but two final states possible, viz.: imprisonment and liberty, doom and bliss, glory and shame, pain and happiness, unbelievers or Christ rejecters have *the same place of punishment as have Satan and his angels.* The only kingdom to which Satan, his angels and unbelievers aspire being lawlessness—rebellion against God and moral chaos—to the regions of endless darkness and doom, where no ray of heaven or the cross ever penetrates, to disturb, He consigns them. Like stars which should pass beyond their centripetal force, to wander forever, so are all the wicked—Satan, his angels and all men and women who pass into such hardness of heart and unbelief as to be beyond the influence of the cross of Christ—"wandering stars for whom the blackness of darkness hath been reserved forever." (Jude 13.) The wicked, by the centrifugal force of their character—Satan, his demons and Christ rejecters—"shall be cast forth into the outer darkness: there shall be the weeping and gnashing of teeth." (Matt. 8: 12; 22: 13.) Having made their lives, like the lives of Satan and his angels, persistently disobedient, and, in the light of their mission, unprofitable, they can but be driven by their antipathy to God where they can never enjoy the light of His beneficent presence: "Cast ye the unprofitable servant into outer darkness: there shall be the weeping and gnashing of teeth." (Matt. 25: 30.) "The soul that sinneth it shall die." (Ezek. 18: 4.) "For the wages of sin is death." (Rom. 6: 23.) "The wicked shall be turned into hell,* and all the nations that forget God." (Psa. 9: 17.)

---

\* The absurdity of the Universalist evasion, in saying hell is the grave, is manifest in that, if this were so no more is threatened the wicked than is the lot of the righteous.

"And whosoever was not found written in the book of life was cast into the lake of fire." (Rev. 20: 15.) "But the fearful, and unbelieving, and murderers, and whoremongers, and sorcerers, and idolaters, shall have their part in the lake which burneth with fire and brimstone: which is the second death." (Rev. 21:8.) "And these shall go away into everlasting punishment." (Matt. 25: 46.) "And the smoke of their torment ascendeth up forever and ever: and they have no rest day nor night." (Rev. 14: 11.) The wicked preferring error to truth, "Upon the wicked he shall rain snares, fire and brimstone; this shall be the portion of their cup." (Psa. 11: 6)

Some people cry out against hell, as being "unreasonable." But, whether we can see the reason or not for "hell," God, sounding the depths of reason, has made hell, and He never does anything conflicting with the highest reason. Hell is to God's government what earthly prisons are to earthly governments. Why, in the latter case, should the lawless be punished and in the former go unpunished? Why should human government, by imprisonment, punish the rebellious, and divine government treat the law-abiding and the rebellious alike? Why should human government discourage lawlessness by punishing the lawless, and God's government encourage lawlessness by taking the righteous and the wicked to heaven?

The Scripture doctrine of eternal punishment is not eternal punishment for only what Satan, his angels and wicked men *have* done, but, eternal punishment for their hardness of heart, placing them beyond the reach of a righteous thought, feeling or purpose—for what they *will continue* forever to be and do—eternal sinners, consequently eternal hell. Jesus will say: "Depart from me, ye that work [not only have been wicked, but are *now* workers of iniquity—present tense] iniquity." (Matt. 7: 23.) As rendered in the Revised Verson, on the weight of MSS. authority, "guilty of an eternal sin." (Mark 3: 29.) As every Greek scholar knows, rightly rendered in the Revised Version: "He that is unrighteous, let him *do* unrighteousness *still;* and he that is filthy, let him be made filthy *still.*" (Rev. 22: 11.) Devils and sinners being hopelessly beyond the reach of righteous thoughts, feelings and purposes, together banished from the presence of Him whom they take delight in shunning and disobeying, banished so far from light and glory into "*outer* darkness" where they are left to forever aggravate, vex and prey on each other, in the kingdom whose only character is moral chaos and darkness—so far from God, from order, from light and glory as to never be disturbed in their darkness, chaos, preying on each other and in their "weeping and gnashing of teeth," by any of the light and restraint of God, His people, or their principles, and, where they can no more disturb the good, or God's kingdom. "There the wicked cease from troubling." (Job. 3: 17.) Looking into that far off "kingdom" of moral and spiritual darkness and chaos, as God from "the great white throne" has thrown a flash of light over it and given us a heavenly and far-reaching vision, what an awful and horrible sight we there see: "Without are the dogs [Universalism has all within], and the sorcerers, and the fornicators, and the murderers, and the idolaters, and every one that loveth and maketh a lie." (Rev. 22: 15.) Here, again, you see the wicked not in hell for only what they *have* done, but for what they *are*, by their own unbelief and hardness, bound to—"*loveth* and *maketh* a lie." Why, my dear reader, as the highest reason and justice demand that earthly governments have their places of punishment, so the highest reason and justice demand a hell for those who by *character*, *habit* and life are *unfit* for the kingdon of order and of light.  Here is the eternal destruction of Satan, his angels and all human souls who have lived and died in defiance of the kingdom of light and order.

> "There is a death whose pang
> Outlasts this fleeting breath;
> O what eternal horrors hang
> Around the second death."

As earthly prisons create respect for authority, fear of disobedience, and, thus, necessary *support to government*, so, by its influence on all finite intelligences, likely on millions of worlds of which we know not, the doom of the devil, his angels and all wicked men and women not only leaves them where they can never darken the kingdom of light or trouble the good, but, by its *example*, it creates, among all created intelligences, higher regard for the authority of the divine government and greater horror for disobedience, and thus supports the eternal kingdom.

On the road to where Satan can never enter.—Heb. 11: 13, 14; Rev. 21: 4.

## CONCLUSION.

Dear reader, together we have gone in our study, following Satan and his angels from heaven where they are cast into this earth; studying their nature; examining their works with horror; and seeing the final destruction of their works and their doom; and of all who continue in the Satanic kingdom. Now, as we part, to meet, may be, no more on earth, suffer one who loves you to implore you to "*prepare to meet thy God.*" Not *your* goodness nor church-membership can save you. Jesus says. "Except a man be born again, he can not see the kingdom of God." (John 3: 3.) The sweetest message that ever fell on mortal ear is: "God so loved the world that he gave his only begotten Son that whosoever believeth in him should not perish, but have everlasting life." (John 3: 17.) Will you receive it? Not to gratify curiosity did I write this book; but that many thousands of dying men and women, reading it, might see themselves without Jesus hopelessly in Satan's kingdom. "The blood of Jesus Christ his Son cleanses us from all sin." (1 John 1: 7.) "Believe on the Lord Jesus Christ, and thou shalt be saved." (Acts 16: 31.) Not to science, logic, philosophy, creeds, churches or ceremonies, however true they may be, and when in their place however useful, but to HIMSELF Jesus invites your weary soul for rest: "Come unto ME, all ye that labor and are heavy laden, and I will GIVE you rest." (Matt. 11: 28.) With a full surrender of soul to Him and trust in His *blood*—His merits—while on your seat, look to Him and you live forever! Dear reader, in pity, love and mercy God pleads with you *now:* "As I live, saith the Lord God, I have no pleasure in the death of the wicked; but that he turn from his way and live: turn ye, turn ye from your evil ways, for why will ye die?" (Ezek. 33: 11.) WHAT SHALL THE ANSWER BE?

www.ingramcontent.com/pod-product-compliance
Lightning Source LLC
Chambersburg PA
CBHW030356170426
43202CB00010B/1397